The Secrets of successful marriage

A Complete Guide To successful marriage

Copyright © 2022 Evans Paul

TABLE OF CONTENT

INTRODUCTION

Family-related difficulties are at the top of churches' and counseling centers' lists of issues to be counseled. Many people have inquiries about the family, but very few seem to have complete responses. However, a man's testimony also includes having a wonderful family or home. A great family or household is the foundation for any success a man or woman will experience in any aspect of life.

When describing Job's virtues, God—the architect of marriage and the family—made sure to expressly include his family in addition to his character qualities and other strengths.

"In the land of Uz, there lived a man by the name of Job. Job was a perfect and upright person who feared God and shunned wickedness. And seven boys and three girls were born to him. This man was the greatest of all the men of the east because he had a very large family, seven thousand sheep, three thousand camels, five hundred yoke of oxen, and five hundred she asses, in addition to his other wealth." - Job 1:1-3

It is clear from this narrative that a man's testimony is incomplete if he doesn't discuss the situation of his family. The basis for overall success is family success. A guy is guaranteed to succeed in all else in life if he succeeds as the head of his family. No matter how successful a person becomes in life, their success will be unsustainable if it is not supported by unquestionable family success. Many big destinies have failed in society as a result of problems with the family structure. It is tasteless and frustrating to achieve social, financial, professional, or professional (even with celebrity and all).

The family was created by God for prosperity, not failure! He demonstrated this by actively participating in the institution of the first marriage, then the family.

And after putting Adam to sleep, the Lord God plucked one of his ribs and sealed up the flesh inside. Then, using the rib that the Lord God had taken from man, he created a woman and brought her to the man. - Gen. 2:21–22

God did not just speak into existence the first marriage like He did the rest of creation. He had a real hand in its establishment.

The joys and benefits God can bring to every aspect of your life through a fulfilling family life are without bounds. The joy of a successful family is contagious. This happiness merely overflows into every aspect of existence. Joy begs for divine intervention, and with that intervention comes "pleasures for evermore" (Ps. 16:11).

The family can be compared to an extremely valued good. The family cannot work effectively until the pertinent raw ingredients are thoroughly processed, just as every product need vital raw materials before it can be made and function well.

According to Joshua 1:8, "This book of the law must not depart out of thy mouth; but thou shalt meditate therein day and night, that thou mayest observe to do according to everything that is written therein: for then thou shalt make thy path prosperous, and thou shalt have excellent success."

The factory for successful families is "this book of the law" or the Bible. There are several ideas in it that, when applied and put into practice, would guarantee success—and not just success, but good success.

Following biblical marriage rules to the letter is essential for a happy home. God wants you to succeed in all facets of life. But neither does it happen by accident nor is it a result of chance. Nothing that is successful can be categorized as an accident since an accident never bears witness.

I have yet to meet a man or woman who rose to the top of their family by accident or who only recently realized their success after 50 years. It never occurs because achievement is not a gift! It was neither a fortunate or accidental outcome. It doesn't just occur. Success in any endeavor, including the family, requires intentional, calculated, and aware action.

However, the reality of God's Word is unaffected by the fact that many people are unhappy, dissatisfied, tired, and failing. The family is set up to succeed! It is necessary to acknowledge this truth in order to accept it. Joshua 1:8's final sentence, "... Then thou shalt have considerable fortune," refers to this very reason.

The only thing you need to do if you're married and your family is going through storms is to put the ideas found in God's Word into practice. By following the guidelines laid out in God's Word, you can prevent frustration if you're preparing to start your own family. However, if your family may be considered "successful," it can go to the level of excellent success! Success needs to be continually improved upon in order to be successful. If success today is not enhanced, it will turn into failure tomorrow. The potential for progress is the biggest space on earth.

Your family will have a brighter tomorrow! You can enjoy God's best because of this, in my opinion, which is why God gave me the command to create this book. For you, I think only the best will do.

CHAPTER 1

EXPLORING THE FAMILY

"As a result, God made both males and females in his image, creating man in the process. They were blessed by God, who also commanded them to reproduce and fill the land." Genesis 1:17–1:28

Because the family is the fundamental unit of every nation, people, tribe, and race, even the tiniest nation, no nation can be better than the wellbeing of the individual families that make up that nation. It serves as the cornerstone of a normal society's social structure.

When asked how to bring about world peace, Mother Theresa, the renowned holy lady of God and founder of the Order of the Missionaries of Charity, responded, "Let everyone go home and love their families." She meant it literally when she said that the misuse and misinterpretation of family structure and values is at the root of the current state of turmoil in the world.

Family as a Unit

According to the Longman's Dictionary of Contemporary English, the word "family" refers to a group of individuals who are intimately linked to one another, particularly the nuclear family, which consists of the mother, father, and children. However, there is also the extended family structure, which consists of distant relatives, grandparents, aunts, and uncles, among others.

The family unit can also be described as two or more individuals who live together typically under one roof or in the same house, share common interests and morals, and have been committed to one another for a significant amount of time.

The Bible also uses the terms "household" and "house of" to refer to families, as in Psalm 115:12. It says: "He will bless the house of Israel; he will bless the house of Aaron," referring to God's desire for the family unit. Furthermore, Genesis 18:19 declares: "For I know him, that he will command his children and his family after him..."

We can observe from this paragraph that the term "household" encompasses more than just the husband, wife, and children because the word "children" was used before the term "household." A household includes much more than simply a husband, wife, and child; it can also refer to everyone who resides there and is subject to the householder's or the home's owner's jurisdiction. Close relatives, distant relatives, in-laws, household workers, and servants are examples of such people (some people have their drivers, gardeners, security personnel, etc., living with them under the same roof, and treat them as members of their family).

The Relationship of Marriage

The legal union of a man and a woman as husband and wife is called marriage. It serves as the cornerstone upon which family members' lives and relationships are started or developed.

According to the demands of the law, tradition, or religion, marriage is a connection between two persons who are already wed or who have been joined as husband and wife. Although one of the benefits of marriage is having children, cohabiting with someone of the opposite sex is not the only benefit of marriage. Marriage is basically a covenant between a man and a woman that unites them in an eternally committed union. It is a two-person commitment and agreement made in front of witnesses. It is a type of relationship that enables a man and a woman to unite as husband and wife, become one flesh, and jointly rule over the globe.

It is the bringing together of two individuals, specifically a man and a woman, a husband and a wife, to make a lifelong commitment to one another and to start a family or construct a home together.

The first marriage is the creation of God.

"And the LORD God thought, It is not right that the man should be alone; I will make him a help meet for him," is what the Bible says in Genesis 2:18.

The verses that follow describe how God carried out that task. God created the woman and gave her to her husband, demonstrating His interest in marriage. He personally attended the first wedding (Genesis 2:12–23)! What else? Jesus transformed water into wine at a wedding in Cana of Galilee, the first miracle He ever worked during His time on earth. This restored the marriage's lost zest and joy (Jn. 2:1-11).

Does your marriage currently seem to lack joy? Do not give up. Because God is still a miracle worker, He will perform a miracle in your life just as He did at Cana. Count on a miracle! But you must be prepared to follow His guidance, just as they did at the Cana wedding before their water was changed into wine. You'll also be blessed twice.

God is the cornerstone of a happy marriage since He created it. He is the foundation for a successful family life, so build yours on Him. While expecting to experience supernatural blessings and benefits in their marriage and family life, many couples ignore God and His principles. That is impossible since God's place in your life determines where you are in life as a whole.

Family versus Marriage

remarked Fredrick K. C. Price: "A divine ordinance, marriage. You cannot have a family without marriage, which is a divine law.

A family cannot reside in a residence with a group of others residing there. You won't have any Christian relationships, but you will have a place to live." In other words, since there must be a marriage in order for a family to be established, there can be no family if there is no marriage. Let everything be done nicely and in order, the Bible commands. First Corinthians 14:40

Although vital to the family unit, the marriage bond is distinct from other family relationships. Watch to see how.

First of all, a marriage unites a man and a woman, a husband and a wife. Only two people of the opposite sex are involved. This fact needs to be made extremely clear, particularly in these "modern" times of "same sex marriages." Same-sex unions might be acceptable in society, but God does not approve of them. For: "He created male and female." in Genesis 1:27 Thus, a man "shall cleave unto his wife." in Genesis 2:24

In the verses above, you'll notice the phrases "male," "female," "man," and "wife." All of these indicate to two people who are of different sexes, not the same sex. God is an intricate God. God's form of marriage requires doing things His way. Things that prevent marriage success. Precaution, Precaution, Precaution! Be not misled, for neither fornicators nor idolaters nor adulterers nor effeminate (homosexuals) nor abusers of themselves with men... shall inherit the kingdom of God, says the word of God. 6:9–10 in 1 Corinthians

Life will turn against you if you reject God's word, The Bible cannot be faltered. To try to dissect the texts is to dissect existence itself. People who mock God's word inevitably become victims in life.

The family, however, consists of at least two and, eventually, more members.

Second, marriage is a commitment between one man and one woman that results in a fusion, a merging, and a lifelong relationship. Covenant governs the relationship between a husband and wife.

Not only is marriage a good concept, but it is also God's idea. It was created by God, hence it is divine. It is a scriptural issue rather than a cultural one. It is a result of God's arrangement rather than one made by man. A familial connection, on the other hand, is a shared ancestoral or associational bond that creates a tether between members of the same family. Its existence is not always of their own free will. In other words, you truly don't get to choose which family you want to be a part of " Judah then declared to his brothers, "He is our brother and our flesh."" Gen. 37:26–27

Thirdly, being married is a conscious decision made by both parties. But whether or not they want to, every member of a family is connected by their shared ancestry.

The marriage you find yourself in is a result of your decisions, and choices are extremely essential. Isaac instructed his son Jacob in Genesis 28:2 to "Arise, go to Padan-aram, to the house of Bethuel, thy mother's father; and take thee a bride from thence, of the daughters of Laban, thy mother's brother." They greatly influence the way our lives are lived.

The family you are born into, on the other hand, is not something you chose. Birth establishes the bond between children and their parents. Before you are born, you are not able to pick your mother or father. Maybe you did? You cannot alter your mother's or your father's characteristics. However, the good news is that God is perfect and never errs. Whatever family you are born into, it was chosen by God specifically for you and is for the best. Never wish you had been born into a different family. It is best for you to fulfill your purpose for existing in the family into which you are born. Be ecstatic! You were born at the proper time.

Never belittle the family you were born into. God might have sent you there, despite the difficulties, at this precise moment. You will succeed in overcoming those obstacles and become a champion.

Fourth, marriage serves as the family's cornerstone. A marriage is voluntarily entered into, and it later develops into a family. The values that uphold a marriage must also guide family members' lifestyle choices. This is so because each person in a marriage makes a decision for himself. However, by starting a family, the person is bringing their loved ones and more people together to share in either the positive environment that is established or the difficult experiences that are being suffered (Gen. 47:9).

It's not meant to be endured, but to enjoy marriage and family.

Maintaining a Family

After marriage, a couple begins their married life or joint experience of life. They no longer lead solitary lives. There have been and continue to be changes. Each party is now required to think about their spouse as well as themselves. After the marriage, other people (connected by blood or by association) and children are added (either by birth or adoption). Then a family is formed. Marriages give rise to families. One flows into another.

Family

A family is a group of people who are related via marriage or blood. It serves as the foundation of both the Church and a country. It is a fundamental social unit in society and normally consists of a husband and wife, together with any children they have together. A marriage is made up of a man and a woman who have common aims and beliefs, are committed to one another for a lifetime, and live together, as opposed to a family, which is made up of a group of people with shared ancestry.

Home Life

A family is a group of people who live together and have a common ancestor. It is the way a family or group of people connected by blood or marriage live together as a household. It is how parents, kids, and other close family members live.

Interestingly, neither a married person nor a single person ever fell to Earth from heaven. Every person on earth, whether they are young or old, wealthy or impoverished, male or female, black or white, originated from a different family and a different lineage, and they all share a genetic or social connection with someone else. Everyone on earth is therefore affected by issues relating to family and family life.

The Family System

Because each house was built by a different man, but God is the one who created everything. Hebrews 3:14

"Every wise lady builds her house," they say. 1 Proverbs 14

In the aforementioned texts, the word "house" does not relate to a physical building but rather to a family structure, or the people who make up the household. Building a home is the responsibility of the individual. By managing the people living beneath your roof, you construct.

"Let the deacons rule (administre) their children and their own homes well, being the husband of one wife." Timotheus 3:12

Effective management is necessary for the family structure. Families that lack this ultimately produce people who undermine and undermine society. Therefore, the purpose of the family is to foster an environment or atmosphere for the efficient management and preparation of individuals so they can develop and successfully pursue God's plan for their lives " ... The dwelling place of the evil will be destroyed, but the habitation of the righteous will grow. There is a generation that does not bless their mother and curses their father (Prov. 14:11; 30:11). "

They assert that "charity begins at home." But it doesn't stop there; that's just where it starts. This suggests that a person's character and destiny should start in their home and develop appropriately from there.

Abraham is a prime biblical illustration of this.

God declared regarding Abraham in Genesis 18:19, "For I know him, that he will command his children and his family after him, and they will observe My way, to do righteousness and judgment; that I may bring upon Abraham that which I have foretold of him."

Abraham was able to manage his household properly because he understood God's plan for the family. God was pleased with him as a result, and he made sure that Abraham and his family were successful in whatever they did. Christians continue to associate themselves with Abraham to this day. Would God say something uplifting about your marriage or family today if He were to comment on it?

Marriage serves as the cornerstone of the family, which in turn serves as the cornerstone of society. Satan consistently seeks to destroy couples. This is because dismantling marriages would also dismantle families, and dismantling families would dismantle the Church, society, and country. But we must stop this from happening.

God made the family the primary and most important unit of human society. The institution of marriage was the first and predated all other institutions. It is the world's oldest institution. God is a priority-oriented God. Before the Church, he established the institution of marriage. Before coming down to associate with man in the cool of the day, He first established marriage (Gen. 2:18- 25; 3:8). The family existed before there were nations, governments, educational institutions, or corporations, and marriage existed before the family. Marriage is the cornerstone upon which society was first erected by God.

Marriage was the foundation for the growth of Adam and Eve's social interaction as they developed together when God brought them together in the garden. They discovered their duties to one another and carried out their commitments to one another in the setting of marriage. The institution of marriage is essential to the survival of human society in all of its manifestations.

Marriage serves as the cornerstone upon which the Church, the body of Christ, and God's unique society are built. According to the New Testament, Christ and His Church have a relationship similar to that of a bridegroom and his bride. Understanding how husbands and wives are to interact with one another is greatly affected by this analogy (Eph. 5:21-23, 25, 31-32). The connection between Christ and His Church serves as an example of what a husband and wife should have: mutual respect, submission to one another, and selfless love. The family, the smallest but yet most fundamental unit of society, is referred to as a "home" throughout the whole Bible, from Genesis to Revelation. The family needs God's assistance now more than ever to be free from the problems, difficulties, and disasters that plague it every day.

A grasp of the family's values is necessary for any house or family to continue standing and endure the test of time, even though every house and family is built by one or both men and women. Every family must also be established and developed according to God's original design and guiding principles.

CHAPTER 2

THE FAMILY IN GOD'S MASTER PLAN

And make sure to follow the blueprint that was provided to you in the mount when creating them. Excodus 25:40

Without a master plan, any physical construction effort will undoubtedly be ineffective. When a master plan is created, all the builders need to do is adhere to it precisely to produce a stunning structure. Therefore, the "map" of a building is the master plan.

You can compare marriage to a house. God is the master plan's architect, and the husband and wife are its builders. In order for them to have a successful marriage and family, they must carefully adhere to the architect's design. For this reason, the Bible explicitly states that "For every home is framed by some man; but he who framed all things is God." (Hebrews 3:4)

An establishment is made through understanding and a house is built through wisdom. (Proverbs 24:3)

A strategy

In His word, God makes it clear what His intentions are for marriage as a union and the family as a unit. Before enjoying the success it entails, this plan must be learned, comprehended, and put into practice. This is abundantly clear from Genesis 2:24, which states, "Therefore a man shall leave his father and his mother, and shall cleave unto his wife, and they shall be one flesh."

Here, Leave, Cleave, and One Flesh stand out as the three most obvious principles. Family success can be attained through the discovery, comprehension, and application of these principles. Let's quickly go over each of them.

Leave

The first rule of God's grand scheme involves leaving home. It is a directive. A man and his wife form a new family unit when they get married; it is distinct from the families that each of them came from.

"Therefore, a man shall leave his father and mother..." Genesis 2:14

The wife is also included in the instruction, even though the husband is specifically told not to leave in this verse. This is because they cannot establish their new home until they both succeed in leaving their current ones. The instruction above is also very detailed. It is stated unequivocally that a man must depart from his father and mother, not his sisters, brothers, uncles, or aunts. Why? That's because a person's parents are their closest blood relatives. If leaving them is possible, it should be much simpler to leave brothers, sisters, uncles, aunts, or any other relative.

While the bond between a parent and child is temporary and thus may be broken, the one between a husband and wife is permanent and should not be.

What then does leaving mean? When used in this context, leaving means gaining parental autonomy. Father, mother, and other family members shouldn't be responsible for managing the new home's daily operations. Instead, the husband and his wife should have complete control over it. It does not imply that parents are no longer involved, but it does imply that the family functions independently of one another. It refers to forbidding the old family—from which both come—from remotely controlling the new family. It should cover every aspect of life. A fundamental idea is this one.

The husband and wife ought to physically depart. A man and his wife should ideally move into their own home after getting married, whether it was purchased, leased, or constructed by them. It doesn't matter how small the house is; what matters is that we obey God's word. It's usually preferable, even if it's just one room at first. For the man and his wife, this makes the transition period easier. As responsible, independent adults, they can live much more comfortably. This is due to the fact that they both need time to spend alone together getting to know one another better.

It is best to avoid situations where a man and his wife, after getting married, continue to reside there physically with either parent. It typically causes relationships to deteriorate. A couple who currently resides in a one-room apartment could move into a mansion in the future. Never mock the days of modest beginnings!

The husband and wife are destined to depart emotionally. God endowed us with emotions. But being able to direct our emotions in the right directions is crucial. Children are emotionally bonded to their parents from birth. After marriage, this emotional attachment to one's parents must be properly managed to prevent emotional breakdowns. Here, maturity is necessary. This further demonstrates the fact that marriage is only for mature people—men and women, not boys and girls—in God's grand design.

Mentally, the couple should distance themselves from their parents. The husband and wife should be prepared to make decisions on their own and take ownership of them. Responsibilities are everything in life! They must both be prepared to consult one another when making decisions. They must be prepared to handle the difficulties of living together. Decisions that directly impact their new family shouldn't be made on their behalf by their parents. Parents should not be held responsible for any poor choices made by their children. Some couples are unable to move forward in their relationship without their parents' blessing. This shouldn't exist. Both of them must depart mentally.

A husband and his wife are expected to part ways with their parents financially as well. They should be self-sufficient financially. Both of them need to be capable of working, making money, and managing their finances. They shouldn't have to spend money on their parents, and their parents shouldn't have to spend money on them. To be financially independent, husband and wife must develop the ability to be happy at each stage of their lives. My husband often argues that just as there are seasons in life, so too are males.

However, a word of warning! Without limiting the aforementioned, a husband and his wife must see to it that they uphold their covenant duties to their parents. It's important to keep in mind what Ephesians 6:2–3 says: "Honor your parents, for this is the first and greatest commandment, with promise; that it may go well with you, and that thou mayest have long life on the earth."

Honour must be accorded to those who deserve it. Recognize the value of your parents. Respect is a seed. You reap what you sow. You reap what you sow to your own parents when you become a parent. There are tradeoffs in life. You must plant the seeds of honor today if you want to reap them tomorrow.

Cleave

Keep in mind the foundational verse for this part.

Therefore, a guy must forsake his mother and father and cling to his wife. in Genesis 2:24

Cleaving is the next essential in God's grand design for a happy marriage and family. What does the term "cleave" mean?

According to the definition of the term "cleave" in the American Heritage Dictionary, it means "to adhere, cling, or stick fast to." In light of this definition, God's master plan calls for husbands and wives to adhere, cling, and stick fast to one another for life.

The definition of cleave is "attached to." This does not imply that they should be physically joined. It denotes a melting of two different people into one, a coming together. Ephesians 5:31 states that a man must leave his father and mother in order to marry his wife, after which the two will become one flesh.

A man and his wife, who had previously lived as two different, unique people, are married; they sever their ties with their parents and commit to each other for the rest of their lives. They are now connected to one another rather than being two independent and different people. This serves as the foundation for a friendship and relationship that will last a lifetime.

Togetherness, connection, and intimacy are the results of this. It promotes harmony. It results in unity—oneness in spirit, soul, and body—in everything. Being one in spirit entails that both parties are spiritually awake and a part of the same spiritual kingdom. In the world of the soul, being one means that, despite their particular distinctions, they are both amenable. Their bodily connection as husband and wife, which is their creative force, is referred to as their "oneness in the world of the body." And, wow, when you're all together, nothing can stop you (Gen. 11:6)! Such a surprise! Therefore, husbands and wives need to be cautious of anything that can cause them to disagree and prevent it from happening.

Arguments, hostility, resentment, bitterness, division, miscommunication, venom, hatred, and the like must not be tolerated since they can drive a husband and wife apart even while they are still residing in the same home. A kingdom that is divided against itself will collapse. Can you picture a marriage in which one partner harbors animosities toward the other from a deep place? Such a house will be the devil's ideal operating environment. Naturally, if you give the devil a place to stay, he will remove you from that location. Confusion is not something God created. Every bad work is present wherever there is misunderstanding (Jms. 3:16).

At this point, I must clarify, however, that there can be no cleaving without first departing. The first has to come first. Cleaving happens after leaving. God is a God of priority and order. It is hard for a man and his wife to cling to one another until they both leave their separate families behind.

It's important to keep in mind that leaving does not always result in cleaving.

There is no automatic cleaving. You don't have to cleave to leave. Loneliness is a huge issue in homes today because of this, which is what causes it. Many marriages have split up, gone their own ways, and ultimately divorced due to loneliness. Cleaving does not automatically occur when two people get married. Never make the assumption. Instead, it needs to be planned for and actively pursued to become reality. A crucial, critical element in making this happen is effective communication. This book will discuss this topic in more detail later on.

One Body

The third tenet of God's grand design is this.

They will become one flesh after that. in Genesis 2:24

Because of this, they are no longer two, but one flesh. 19:6 in Matthew

And they will become one flesh. in Ephesians 5:31

A husband and wife are one flesh in God's eyes! This must be the origin of Adam's statement in Genesis 2:23 that his wife was "now bone of my bones, and flesh of my flesh: she shall be named Woman, for she was taken out of Man" when he first saw her.

In a marriage, one man and one woman make up one flesh. This math is from God! This alludes to the merging of the husband and wife, two separate components into one. At this moment, they can no longer be "disjoined"; they become inseparable. It has developed into a lifetime commitment. Nothing but a great mystery exists here! Ephesians 5:32, a verse from the Bible, attests to this.

An unfathomable reality that can only be known through divine revelation and confounds human logic is referred to as a mystery. You can command dominance on earth when you comprehend, put into practice, and live by God's mysteries. When you comprehend and put into practice God's marriage mysteries, you may overcome any marital difficulties.

The peculiar bond between a husband and wife is mysterious. Marriage is a mystery because it demonstrates how two individuals from various origins, with diverse wills, preferences, and life experiences, can coexist in a committed partnership and learn to adapt to, complement, and balance one another. Even though it's hard to explain, this exists.

God did not create marriage to cause pain, but to help man be free from all types of misery so he can become master of his own life. In the name of Jesus, I see your freedom from every sorrow in life established as you obey God's design for marriage. I also see you gaining mastery.

One Flesh's Mysteries

There are a lot of lessons to be drawn from this. Let's look at a few of them.

Treat your spouse with respect.

Understanding the concept of "one flesh" will change how husbands and wives interact with one another. Don't subject your partner to something you wouldn't do to yourself. Treat your partner the way you would like to be treated. Take care of your partner the way you would like them to take care of you.

You must treat your partner with kindness and not with cruelty if you want them to be good to you. Do the same first if you desire your spouse's respect. You get back what you put in. If you don't want to experience abuse in return, don't abuse your spouse. Marriage will return to you what you put into it.

Because nobody has ever hated their own flesh; instead, they nourish and cherish it, just like the Lord the church. in Ephesians 5:29

According to The American Heritage Dictionary ""To nourish" is defined as "to supply with food or other materials required for life and growth; feed. promote, encourage development of." It outlines "To "treat with compassion and affection; hold dear" is to "celebrate." to cherish in the mind."

A husband and wife should support one another, encourage one another, show one another affection and tenderness, hold one another in high regard, and think of one another with fondness. To be able to do this, one must comprehend the mystique of one flesh.

Don't Provide For Divorce.

Make every effort to stay married.

As a result, "pay heed to your spirit, that ye deal not treacherously," says the LORD, the God of Israel, "for I despise putting away, for one covers violence with his garment, said the LORD of hosts." Matthew 2:16

God abhors storage! You should despise anything that God hates. Nothing should be used to tear apart what God has bonded together (Matt. 19:5-6; Mk.10:9).

Divorce should not be your first course of action when facing a crisis in your marriage. Instead, it's critical to first recognize and assess the difficulty. Make suggestions after that, and pick a potential resolution. Almost all issues can be resolved in this way.

You can never overcome what you don't face head-on. Make a

commitment to solving problems rather than ignoring them. If you go to bed with issues, you'll still have them waiting for you when you wake up!

Divorce is like having your marriage amputated. It brings forth a great deal of sorrow, agony, and wounds that only God can mend. Even after a wound has healed, a scar usually lasts a lifetime. Avoid making divorce arrangements. Keep in mind that prevention is always preferable to treatment.

Even if a man has an artificial replacement for a missing body part, the distinction still exists. The fact that a portion of this man's body has been severed may go unnoticed by others who approach him from a distance, but the person who is concerned cannot claim ignorance!

See what the text says: "...Moses suffered you to put away your women because of the hardness of your hearts, but it was not thus from the beginning." Matt. 19:8

"And I order the married, but it is not I, but the Lord. Do not let the wife leave her husband, and do not let the husband confine his wife." First Corinthians 7:10

Therefore, God's original design for marriage did not include divorce. The high divorce rate in our day and age is one of the worst tragedies. Always terrible and devastating, divorce. One of the biggest problems our society is currently facing is the dissolution of the family. Not to mention the ruined lives of children who experience instability and devastation, the partners go through unimaginable suffering. God considers spouses and wives as having been permanently joined together, and nothing should be permitted to break them apart.

Perhaps you are reading this book and considering divorce because you feel there is no other option. Just wait! Who knows, maybe this is why God gave you the chance to read this book. Your tale will improve if you merely accept and carry out God's grand design.

Do you already have a divorce? Do not let your bright future be destroyed by a sense of condemnation. God restores things. Do you realize that a miracle can yet happen in your life and family to restore things? God restores things!

And I will give you back the years that the caterpillar, the cankerworm, the caterpillar, and the palmerworm have devoured. -Joel 2:25

There should be no divorce, in general. However, if you've already been divorced, God meets you there. If you've since remarried, God has accepted your current union as legally binding. Ask God's pardon and then move on from what you did in the past. Regardless of how you ended up in this marriage, God wants you to remain in it right now. Make it a biblical connection, please.

I have read a research conclusion that said divorced persons typically pass away earlier than those who remain married. You won't pass away too soon; rather, you'll live out your days. Divorce is expensive, and if you avoid it, only you will gain.

Let me now state unequivocally that God is a God of second chances. Do not spend your life with a sense of condemnation if you must or have undergone divorce. Make things right with God and with people. Make sure that your current marital situation won't prevent you from spending eternity with God. You are now prepared to fully enjoy life.

Share each other's bodies with each other.

Wives and husbands should practice sharing their physical bodies. Following marriage, the husband's physical body belongs to the wife, and the wife's body belongs to the husband. They are to both take pleasure in each other's bodies. They are no longer required to keep their bodies apart from one another. Take note of what I Corinthians 7:4-5 says in the Bible:

"The wife has no control over her own body; instead, the husband does; and vice versa for the husband as well. Do not defraud one another."

Man and wife, understand that your physical union is your creative power. God created sex, and it is a key part of our lives. It is meant to be enjoyed exclusively by a husband and his wife after marriage. This physical union is what produces children. Sex is to be enjoyed, not endured. Don't use it to punish your spouse!

In marriage, sex is the ultimate in oneness between a husband and wife. Your sex life affects your attitude positively or negatively. Sexual tension is the foundation of crises in many marriages and homes, but it can be avoided. My husband says when a marriage lacks romance it starts suffering disintegration. God created sex specifically for husbands and wives to enjoy. The Bible has sexual content. It is more straightforward on the human sex desire than many previously produced manuals and talks about it honestly (Judges 14:1-2). After all, God presented a naked Eve to a naked Adam! Therefore, a husband and wife shouldn't be embarrassed to see one other naked.

Sex in marriage is solely a giving act, hence it should only be utilized when it is appropriate in God's grand design. There is a replica for anything that is authentic. Satan wants to corrupt sexuality. Use your body appropriately with your spouse as a husband or wife, not for bad or selfish reasons. Never, for instance, give your spouse your body in exchange for something from them. Never prostitute your body when married; this is perverse sex!

When a husband and wife are genuinely one in body, it is simple to resist external temptations. Keep in mind that only during marriage is sex appropriate. Sex is sinful outside of marriage (I Cor. 6:9). It is the scarlet sin, and it sinks destinies, in reality! Your fate won't sink, I promise!

Therefore, if you adhere to God's ultimate plan for marriage, you will undoubtedly succeed despite the devil. God created families and marriage to be successful. Marriage is supposed to bring happiness and mutual pleasure to both parties. Men and women have cherished their marriages and families since the days of the Bible.

However, you might assert that every family has its own problems based on your personal experience and that of those around you. Nothing is more false than that. For instance, just because you have a headache does not mean that everyone else does as well. Here on earth, it is entirely possible to live a family life without incident. When I searched the scriptures, I discovered examples of people who had trouble-free family lives through their encounters and testimonies, which I used to support my claim. Let's quickly review a few of them:

NOAH

Come into the ark with your entire household, the LORD commanded Noah. You are the first righteous person this generation that I have seen. Genealogy 7:1

The first family to stand out in a generation of wickedness after the fall of man was Noah's. In the midst of the devastation, God singled him and every member of his family out because he had been so successfully married.

Knowing that a man can be successful in family life even before the dispensation of grace is great. That is to say, a man has already gained God's favor by his dedication to his family before the time of Jesus and the age of grace.

However, Noah "received favor in the sight of the LORD." Genealogy 6:8

You and I have no justification for failing to succeed in our families if Noah could succeed. Jesus already paid the full price, so your family has no reason to feel pressure, anxiety, or aggravation.

He was the ideal stand-in for us. In order for us to experience glory and honor in our homes, he was wounded, bruised, beaten, humiliated, spat on, etc. Because of this, a guy has no justification for hitting his wife. not one at all! A man who beats himself must be mentally unstable. In the same spirit, only a guy out of his mind would physically abuse his spouse in marriage because a husband and his wife are one flesh (Mk.10:8)

ABRAHAM.

Abraham, the founder of the nations, had a happy marriage. Abraham was devoted to his barren wife during those times when the law had not yet been given. He had a happy marriage even before he became God's friend. His devotion to and relationship with God did not lessen, but rather strengthened, his dedication to his family.

He was a man that God could trust to tell his family to obey Him. If we really are Abraham's offspring, then "like father, like son" should apply to us. Look at Abraham, your father, and Sarah, your mother, for I called him alone, blessed him, and enlarged him, according to Isaiah 51:2.

It is time to dress and behave like our forefather Abraham, not only to live a life of faith but also to be faithful in raising our families in accordance with God's plan. Remind yourself that you wouldn't have issues with your family if Abraham didn't. It's about time you started following in your father's footsteps. Abraham succeeded, so you will too!

PETER

The mother of Peter's wife was lying in bed and suffering from a fever when Jesus entered Peter's home. Her illness subsided when he touched her hand, and she got up to serve them. - Matthew 8:14–15

Simon A successful married man, Peter was one of the most important apostles and Jesus' right-hand man when He was on earth. Since there is no record of Peter's wife or any of his children ever confronting him on the crusade grounds for failing to uphold his marital duties, there is no reason to question whether or not he was a happy marriage.

He enjoyed tranquility at home, and I think that was a big part of why he could complete his course with joy. Neither his ministry nor his marriage were a barrier to one another. We need to draw a lesson from this for gospel ministers. Having a troubled marriage or family cannot be justified by your work in the ministry. Nobody has a legitimate excuse for failing if Peter could succeed despite Jesus' hectic schedule.

Only fools doubt proofs, and these demonstrate that family success is a fact. Because God's word provides the blueprint for a successful marriage, we have a duty to conform to its precepts. With this comprehension of God's grand design, get ready to start building a successful family life that is free from failure, pressure, shame, and ineffectiveness.

CHAPTER 3

WHY DO FAMILIES SUCCEED?

Success in life, especially in marriage, does not happen by accident. It results from proper adherence to the truth of God's word. Nobody ever claims that an accident was successful. Nobody succeeds by accident. A happy marriage is not something that just happens; it is created. Many people dream of success, but some individuals actually get up and work for it, according to a wise guy. Your impression of the family is the first step in determining whether or not your family is successful.

Every item in existence serves a purpose, and families are no different. Power is in purpose! The right family structure and values will be kept, treasured, and reinforced when the family's mission is well understood.

The temptation to mistreat, exploit, and take for granted this crucial institution, which forms the backbone of every nation and people, results from a lack of understanding and appreciation for what the family is and what it stands for.

Why Do Families Exist?

The family, why? What justifies the existence of this thing?

For every house is constructed by a guy. Hebrews 3:14

The verse above reveals God's intention for families: "Every house is built by some man." Families and households are relationships designed to help each person become their best selves. The lives of the people who comprise a family or household are supposed to go through a building process. The God-ordained setting for such a building process is the family. But because of poor family foundations, family members have only been partially developed, which always leads to societal and national degeneration.

The family setting is the setting God intended for such training. Values must be taught and character qualities must be ingrained among family members. That house or family cannot be built up, and neither can that nation be established, without a clear understanding of what the family and home are meant to be (a place and environment for developing godly and strong character in individuals, a place to develop people prepared to provide loving and selfless service). A house divided against itself cannot stand, according to the Lord Jesus (Matt.12:25).

It is crucial that you have a clear understanding of what the family represents and understand what its creator, God, had in mind when He formed it. This knowledge will enable you to evaluate your own family.

As we've seen, the word "home" in the Bible refers to the family, which is the smallest and most fundamental part of society. We have also proven that any society is built on the foundation of the home, and that every home's original foundation is laid by marriage. This means that every country's or society's health depends on how well its families are doing, and how well those families are doing depends on how well the marriages that support those families are doing.

Families that are successful and stable don't just happen. They need to be built on a solid marriage foundation in order to function correctly. The right foundation begins with the union of a man and a woman, following which children are born. The cohabitation of unmarried men and women, persons of the same sex, or unwed mothers and babies is not a suitable basis on which to create a family.

The Bible forbids using an unsound foundation. What can the virtuous do if the foundations are demolished, according to this verse in Scripture? -Psalm 11:3

If the family foundation is flawed, the result will be flawed people in society, which will finally bring about everyone's sorrow.

Even if some people believe that whether a Christian couple succeeds in marriage or not is none of anyone's business, every Christian couple should strive for success in their marriage and family life. That is false, especially given that many couples are unaware of the profound effects that the success or failure of a family, especially a Christian family, can have.

Has The Family Got To Win?

How do we know that God intended the family to be successful? Let's take a quick look at this issue. The Lord God prompted... And when Adam slept, the Lord God put him into a deep sleep. Then, the Lord God removed one of his ribs and sealed up the flesh inside. From that rib, the Lord God created a woman and brought her to the man. Genesis 2:12–22

The very first wedding ceremony is described in this chapter of Genesis. God played a direct role in the establishment of the first family ever. Like He did with the rest of creation, God did not just speak it into existence; rather, He created Adam. After putting him to sleep soundly, he removed a rib from his side. He created the woman from this rib and gave her to Adam.

Thus, the creator was none other than God Himself. Therefore, marriage has its roots in divinity. Anything connected to God is, without a doubt, destined for success. Given that God is involved, marriage is destined for prosperity.

Be prolific, he commanded. "As a result, God made both males and females in his image, creating man in the process. And God blessed them, telling them to procreate, multiply, replenish the land, and conquer it, as well as to exercise dominion over all other living things on the planet, including fish in the water, birds in the air, and other animals." Genesis 1:17–1:28

God did not start the human family with a curse but

with a blessing. Be prolific, multiply, replenish the earth, and dominate it, he commanded Adam and Eve. These are such beautiful blessings! Beyond reproduction, fruitfulness also refers to prosperity in all spheres of life. It also signifies achieving a lot of success. Every family is destined for success, as evidenced by the fact that God showered the first family with blessings. In the name of Jesus, these blessings will answer for you!

Have Dominance...

"...have dominion over every living thing that moves upon the land, over the fish of the sea, over the birds of the air." 1:28 in Genesis

The family was founded to have dominion, that is, to have and exercise control, according to the American Heritage Dictionary's definition of "dominion." It was decided that it would be in charge of life's circumstances rather than being subject to them. This alone is evidence that it was designed for success.

He Added Them To Eden.

The man was then taken by the LORD God and placed in the Garden of Eden to maintain and care for it. Genesis 2:15.

Because of where God put the family, it is clear that they were intended for success. You will understand that Eden was not a wilderness if you have read the description of it. In actuality, it literally means tremendous joy or delight.

The first couple was put in a happy spot by God. He wants you to enjoy being with your family. All members of the family should have fun together, feel content, laugh, and be excited. He never wanted the family to feel under strain, only happy. He created families so that life would be enjoyable. As you read this book, if your family's situation is anything but pleasant, trust God for a change, and it will happen for you!

They Did Not Feel Shame

The man and his wife were both naked and did not feel embarrassed. in Genesis 2:25

God created marriage to prevent man from ever feeling ashamed. Man's state of better living, glory, and beauty was brought about by marriage. There was no reason to be afraid or sorry. To remove your shame is the third reason God established the family, one of many reasons He created it to succeed. You won't recognize shame any longer!

This Beginning of Miracles...

"This beginning of miracles did Jesus in Cana of Galilee, and manifested forth his glory; and his disciples believed on him." - John2:11

It is absolutely awesome to discover that the first miracle ever performed by Jesus during His earthly ministry was at a wedding ceremony. God is a God of priorities, who would always put first things first. By this miracle, He put a stamp of approval on the need for success in the family.

At this particular wedding, the wine had finished. The wine here represents joy. Jesus then stepped in, instructed them on what to do, they obeyed and thus had more wine than at the onset of the wedding.

The family is ordained of God to be a miracle centre! Many have and are still enjoying miracles in their marriages and families This teaches that marriages experience continuous joy and fulfillment when they obey God's word. Shame is also eliminated. The time for your miracle has arrived, and your shame is over!

Effects of an unhappy marriage

So what are the effects of an unhappy marriage? What occurs when a marriage between two people is unsuccessful?

It Has an Impact on Your Christian Testimony

Since you are the reason that the name of God is profaned among the Gentiles. Romans 2:14

When a Christian family struggles, it provides unbelievers a platform to defame God. Your Christian testimony is precisely what is being harmed when your unbeliever neighbors witness you and your wife arguing and fighting every day, calling your kids various derogatory names, or when they see your kids acting in ways that are characteristic of what the Bible calls "unruly." Given that they are aware of your family's condition, how can you welcome them to church or share your testimony with them? In your family, there is nothing to aspire to.

How can you expect the people around you who aren't Christians to accept your Christian testimony as a man if you don't fulfill your covenant obligations in the house, such as providing for basic needs of life? What kind of evidence does a guy have if he departs town just as his wife is ready to put the kids to bed or his wife is about to start school and he makes no provisions at all for them? These have a detrimental effect on his Christian testimony.

It slows down prayerful responses.

For the same reason, "you husbands, dwell with them according to understanding, paying honor to the wife, as unto the weaker vessel, and as being heirs jointly of the grace of life; that your prayers be not hindered." -1 Peter 3:7

The quickest method to prevent you from receiving answers to your prayers is to have discord in your Christian home. Keeping this in mind, prayer is simply talking to God. Try as you might, your prayer will be hampered if your household is in chaos.

Every Christian needs the unique connection to God that is developed as we spend time in contact with Him. Your relationship with God is also impacted when you and your spouse or other family members are always at odds. Remember that the entire globe is in God's gaze. He therefore observes your arguments with your spouse, and you then go to church to pray and socialize. God can't be tricked; He won't be mocked.

In Jesus' name, the channel of communication between you and God won't be cut off when you mend fences with your relatives.

Your donations are ineffective.

Therefore, "Leave there your gift before the altar and go thy way; first be reconciled to your brother, and then come and offer your gift," if you bring your offering to the altar and realize that your brother has something against you. in Matthew 5:23–24

This explains why many Christians give so much while experiencing such little in return. At home, they argue and fight, and then they bring their gifts to the altar and hope for success. Giving is pointless until there is sanctity within the household. Even if God were in need, no human being could satisfy those demands since God is not in need! He is the source of all our sustenance. Hear this: Your husband and other members of your household are your first neighbors. Therefore, make sure your family is at harmony if you want God to respect the seeds you have sown. Your donations mean nothing unless it happens.

It Affects Your Children's Future

Children growing up in such families are significantly impacted by family discord. The main reason for this is that, according to a wise man, "one ounce of example is worth far more than a ton of preachment" for a child.

Your kids are paying attention whenever you argue and fight. They'll question you one day about your sincerity as a born-again Christian. However, you must also be aware that everything your marriage entails now might be imitated in their families tomorrow. After a long day, kids resemble their parents. Would you want your kids to do what you're doing right now? That should give you some ideas! Are you brave enough to ask your kids to follow you as you follow God? If they followed your example, wouldn't they miss heaven?

Do not allow your lack of dedication to your family's prosperity to hinder your children in the future. Those kids may be young now, but they are the generation of the future. Never underestimate your kids because they are well aware of what occurs in your bedroom late at night. Beware! May your children carry on a Christian legacy from you, and may they have wonderful memories of you!

Let me make it absolutely clear before I wrap up this chapter: God created marriage and the family to succeed. But each marriage partner must contribute for this success to materialize. Family prosperity primarily benefits man, not God. You are the one who will gain from your marriage's success or lose out if it doesn't. You'll prevail!

CHAPTER 4

ESTABLISHING A STRONG FOUNDATION

"What can the virtuous do if the foundations are destroyed?" – Psalm 11:3.

A structure's foundation determines how sturdy it is. Because of this, some structures crumble despite having magnificent architectural designs. Nothing can fully replace the requirement for a strong foundation. The household is not forgotten. The strength of its basis will determine its success.

The time leading up to the wedding might be viewed as the family's construction phase. The quality of the courting, the selection of a life mate, and other factors all affect how happy a marriage will be.

I'll be talking about a few very fundamental, very elementary principles here. But take note, there is profundity in its simplicity. These rules must be followed because failure is possible without a clear grasp on them. Let's take a careful look at them.

Wed a Christian.

"Don't be unequally yoked with unbelievers because there is no communion between righteousness and unrighteousness. What relationship does light have with darkness? And how does Christ get along with Belial? or what relationship does a believer have with an unbeliever?" 2. Corinthians 6.14–15

Here, the phrases "fellowship," "communion," and "concord" stand out clearly. Let's briefly examine each of these words in more detail. Sharing comparable interests, values, or experiences is referred to as fellowship. It refers to equals with comparable interests. Concord refers to harmony or mood or interest agreement. The act or occurrence of exchanging ideas or emotions is referred to as communion.

These three letters convey a singular and unmistakable idea: "togetherness." You'll discover that the words "fellowship," "communion," and "concord" encapsulate the essence of marriage. Marriage is a mystery connection of two separate people who come together in a unique covenant relationship; remove any one of these three elements, and it will fail. In this sense, a marriage is all about unity.

If building a successful family is your priority as a Christian, you must make sure you marry a fellow Christian. You will be building a strong foundation in this manner.

Real friendship, communion, or harmony cannot exist between a saved person and an unbeliever. This is primarily due to the basic differences between the lives and characters of those who are saved and those who are not. "How do I recognize the difference between them?" I overhear someone asking. By their fruits, you can tell the difference (Matthew 7:20)!

There is no meeting place between a Christian and a sinner. The foundation of any successful marriage is a personal relationship with Jesus (Col.1:13) (Gen. 24:3). Christian marriages to non-Christians are forbidden by Scripture. Marriage between two people must necessarily be between members of the same spiritual kingdom (Amos 3:3). Abraham, the father of the religion, was fully aware of the significance of his son marrying among his brethren rather than with anyone. "But you shall go to my country and to my family, and take a wife for my son Isaac," he commanded. - Gen. 24:4.

You are not allowed to marry a stranger under the Abrahamic covenant; you must choose a spouse from among your own own. We must follow suit like Abraham's descendants. Christian men and women frequently give in to parental, financial, or social influences. No of the source of the pressure, though, you must resolve that nothing will persuade you to get into a romantic relationship with an atheist. That is the same as constructing on a weak foundation! Such a structure will quickly fall apart like a house of cards. Beware!

Once someone questioned me: "A Christian man has proposed to me and asked for my hand in marriage. Even if I am aware that he is not born again, can't I still proceed to marry him in the hopes that he will become reborn once we are wed?"

You are not the Holy Spirit, therefore don't be fooled into thinking that you may wed an unbeliever with the purpose of converting them after the wedding. By marrying a non-Christian, a Christian disobeys God's word and builds their home on shaky ground.

If you are a single Christian in a relationship with an atheist, you must end it right away to prevent your destiny from being hindered! Your destiny won't be changed! You should never try to keep the connection going by telling yourself, "I'll simply go to church and get the union blessed." You are inviting conflict! You cannot mock God; you will receive what you sow (Gal. 6:7).

Only Christians may be married. It is a straightforward yet extremely effective principle. The lives of Christians and non-believers are vastly different from one another. They both belong to two different spiritual kingdoms. Regardless of the person in question's riches and status, the truth remains that unless you belong to the same spiritual kingdom, your home is being built on a weak foundation.

In the verses that follow, we see how the richest and wisest king of Israel missed it at the conclusion of his life because he disregarded this crucial truth.

"And Solomon's intellect was superior to that of all the eastern country's offspring and all of Egypt. He was wiser than other people, including Ethan the Ezrehite, Heman, Chalcol, and Darda, the sons of Mahol, and he was well-known throughout the world." -1 Kings 4:30-31

So, in terms of wealth and intellect, King Solomon was superior to all other monarchs on earth. Kings 10:23

The Bible states in 2 Chronicles 8:11 that Solomon built the daughter of the Pharaoh a separate residence distant from the City of David because it was a holy place. This implies that Solomon was aware that his marriage to the daughter of the pharaoh was an unholy union " Solomon said, "My wife shall not reside in the house of David, King of Israel, since the places are sacred, whereunto the ark of the Lord hath come," and he carried the daughter of Pharaoh up from the city of David to the house he built for her."

As predicted, Solomon's wives caused him to lose his devotion to God as he grew older. You must exercise prudence and use caution! "For it came to pass, when Solomon was old, that his wives led his heart away after other gods, and his heart was not faultless with the Lord his God, as was the heart of David his father," I Kings 11:4 says.

The tale is related of a guy who prayed to God all night long to give His blessing to his decision to wed an atheist. Kenneth Hagin, a famous man of God, questioned him about his prayers after the all-night service. When he realized what it was, he let the man know that he didn't need to spend the entire night praying for something that wasn't God's will.

Some believers struggle because they want to convince God to endorse actions that are against His will. But it is impossible to control God. Whatever is against His will will never receive His approval. Anything that does not have God's blessing is doomed from the start.

Become A Fruitful Christian

Prosperous individuals produce successful families. According to

Genesis 2:19, "And the Lord God fashioned every beast of the field and every bird of the air out of the earth; and brought them before Adam to see what he would call them: and whatsoever Adam called every living thing, that was the name thereof."

In essence, before giving Adam a woman, God set him a task to test how successful he would be at it. Marriage is about taking charge. There was no guarantee that Adam could handle the additional duty of a family if he couldn't handle the obligation of naming the animals. When Adam completed that task successfully, God added a wife as a gift, favor, and blessing to him.

You cannot succeed in marriage as an individual unless you have achieved success as an individual. For instance, the likelihood that you will develop these habits after marriage is slim if, as a single person, you find it difficult to pray, study God's word, attend fellowship, or serve in the kingdom; if your heart is not panting after God.

This is especially true when you consider that you have more or less free time when you are single because you do not have to take care of a family. So you can be more effective in the kingdom of God.

"But I would have you without carefulness. He that is unmarried careth for the things that belongs to the Lord, how he may please the Lord: But he that is married careth for the things that are of the world, how he may please his wife." - 1 Corinthians 7:32-33

Many Christians consider that success in marriage is simply reliant upon marrying the proper person. Much more than this is the fact that family success is reliant on being the proper person. Get serious with God, and be as good as the person you want to marry.

For instance, if you as a Christian brother desire to marry a virgin, are you a virgin yourself? If as a Christian lady you desire to marry a pastor, become a "pastor material". Remember that water will always seek its own level. They say that similar birds will flock together. Always, like breeds like. You attract people who are like you, not the other way around. Nobody who is a sincere Christian will desire a connection with someone who is not. Because he or she is aware of your spiritual condition, he or she may bind the devil and cast out the vision even if they have a vision and hear a voice introducing you as their life partner.

When you are not serious with God yourself, it will be pointless to continue fasting and praying for a woman who will obey God, "bombarding" the gates of heaven day and night. If you first make your ways acceptable to God, He will merely add the blessing of a bride to you.

But put God's kingdom and righteousness first, and everything else will be added to you. – Matt. 6:33

My husband used this as his platform to find a wife—me, of course! He simply put his life into God's work after learning this verse, and God added a wonderful home for him. The sweeter your own testimony will be!

The Tool for Your Decision

I learned from my studies that people choose their life partners based on three dimensions: the physical, soulish (emotional, intellectual, and spiritual), and the spiritual. They believe they have found their mate after they feel a connection or unity with someone in one, two, or all three of these areas. Let's quickly review each of these.

Wholeness Of The Flesh

Physical gratification is the lifeblood of this relationship. When two people have a physical or fleshly union, some people decide to get married. For instance, you might say to a young man or woman, "Oh, she's gorgeous, or Oh, he's handsome. Look at her physique and skin tone." The physical appearance is the only thing that has drawn your attention. While there is nothing inherently wrong with this type of attraction, it is the wrong foundation upon which to build a relationship that will last a lifetime. People change over time, which many people have a tendency to forget. A man who has broad shoulders, a flat stomach, and a lot of muscle today might develop a pot belly, a flabby belly, and baldness tomorrow. If your love for someone is solely based on how they look, it will wane as their appearance changes. In light of this, the marriage of a husband and wife cannot be sustained on this basis. We must exercise prudence.

The Soul's Unity

The soulish platform, which incorporates the emotions, intellect, and will, is the second foundation upon which many people base their mate selection. You might come across a woman who shares your logic. You two have similar tastes in music, dancing, theater, etc. You therefore speculate, "Maybe she would make a fine wife." You believe that you two are "compatible."

Another possibility is that you meet someone and instantly fall in "love" with them after just one glance. You decide to be married after having deep feelings for the person. Relationships shouldn't be based solely on the unity of the soul because preferences evolve throughout time. Things you enjoy doing today can seem juvenile to you tomorrow, or you might just grow bored with them.

However, feelings can change quickly. You often hear about people who have fallen in love before breaking it off. Keep in mind that even numbers can shift. Therefore, even while it's important to share common interests, have comparable likes and dislikes, and feel a strong emotional attraction to one another, these factors shouldn't be the main driver behind getting married.

The spiritual unity

Because all men are spiritually dead apart from Christ, the most crucial unity that must exist between a man and a woman—and which will also decide how much the marriage flourishes—

is that of the spirit. This can only occur between two born-again Christians. A person is considered to have been "born-again" when his or her spirit, which had previously perished in Adam, has now undergone rebirth.

The fundamental spiritual issues outlined in Hebrews 6:1-2 are agreed upon when there is unity of the spirit. This means that not just any Christian will do. See if you two can agree on key theological matters and guiding principles.

The foundation of repentance from dead deeds, confidence toward God, the theology of baptisms, the laying on of hands, the resurrection of the dead, and eternal judgment should not be laid again as we go toward perfection. -Heb. 6:1-2

Do you agree with the following in essence:

• The doctrine of baptisms (Holy Ghost and immersion by water) • The laying on of hands (either for impartation or healing) • The resurrection of the dead (or is he/she a Sadducee) • Repentance from dead works • Faith toward God

• Everlasting judgment

Adding to that list is: Do you share the same direction of travel? Do you have the same vision or calling? Are there any more doctrines that his or her church upholds? Are you familiar with them and at ease around them?

The spiritual dimension is the most crucial of these, and I've seen that when the spiritual is strong, even when the physical and soulish aren't completely satisfied, the other dimensions also find contentment. The demands of the soul and the flesh are also marvelously addressed when you get married based on the union of the spirit!

One of Lester Sumrall's books that I once read detailed how he met his wife. His flesh allegedly informed him, "This lady is gorgeous," the moment he first met his wife (paraphrased). Then, when they conversed, he realized that they had a lot of soulful traits and thought similarly about a wide range of life's difficulties. But her commitment to, loyalty to, and steadfast love for the ways of God was the primary factor in his decision to marry her. Before his wife passed away and went to live with the Lord, they had been blissfully married for approximately 50 years.

I also went through something quite similar. I thought my spouse was a really gorgeous man when I first met him. I received a voice inside saying, "This is the man!" In addition, we shared the same viewpoints on a variety of life's concerns and still do. But most importantly, it was his spiritual qualities—dedication and unshakeable commitment to Christ and His kingdom—that actually brought us together and contributed to the kind of success we have experienced in our marriage to this day.

And what's this? When we first met, he was actually traveling and serving the kingdom. We first met and decided to get married about twenty-eight years ago, and we've actually been married for about twenty-two years at this point, and it just keeps getting better and better!

Create a courtship When two individuals decide to be married, there is a time called "purposeful courtship" before they really do. A successful courtship is a prerequisite for a happy marriage. Due to a lack of a deliberate courtship, many people encounter misunderstandings and other types of marital problems.

Certain elements improve the standard of your courtship.

Talk to each other for some time.

You must set aside time to spend with your fiancé(e), during which you can share information about each other, such as your goals, interests, points of view, calling or assignment, etc., in order to ensure a quality courtship. This is why it's crucial to converse with each other and not just look at each other and say, "Oh, you are so lovely. I adore you a lot."

Your words are a reflection of your thoughts and where you are headed. If you want to know if he is a serious Christian, listen to him talk for five minutes. I discovered that it is impossible to separate an individual from his words.

If your fiancé(e), for instance, only talks about money, it is an indication that he or she is money minded. If on the other hand he is only interested in your physique, you will hear him speak of nothing else. Your words are an outflow of the thoughts of your heart.

"How can ye, being evil, speak good things? for out of the abundance of the heart the mouth speaketh." -Matthew 12:34

“My husband and I courted for six years (very short, isn't it?), and every time I heard him speak, I knew the direction he was heading. I knew his convictions, which were my convictions also. This made it simple for the two of us to move as one. ” said a friend

Make a Public Show of Force

This is another straightforward yet important component. You must schedule time to appear at public meetings as engaged couples. Church services, weddings, commencement and matriculation ceremonies, open lectures, academic seminars, etc. are a few examples of these public gatherings. I also advise you to keep an eye on each other's behavior while you both emerge in public together. How your future partner handles problems, including his behaviors or responses to irksome circumstances. This will serve as a sign of what lies ahead. For instance, being married to someone who lacks Christian character can only get you into difficulty. If you learn that you are embarrassed to be seen with your prospective husband or wife in public for any social reason, such as height, age, educational differences, physical defects, personal carriage, eating manner, etc., and you don't handle it during courtship, you may never become a decent couple. Be honest and don't go through the wooing process blindly!

Letters should accompany a courtship

In a typical courtship, letters should be exchanged. A letter is only a written or printed message addressed to a specific individual. Writing letters is among the simplest ways to communicate when courting. This comes in very handy, particularly if the parties involved are from different cities or towns.

Even if there are other ways to communicate, such cellphones and the like, letters are still a more respectable form of doing so, particularly in these days of rapid electronic media change. These letters could be sent by mail or by any other method.

Letters have a number of advantages over other forms of communication during this time. For instance, it forces you to logically arrange your thoughts. You are able to arrange your thoughts in a presentable way because you have the chance to read it several times before delivering it.

Second, it develops into a document that may be saved, preserved, and stored for future use and references if necessary. This also instills a great deal of restraint and care, particularly in relation to the content and the likelihood that a third party will view it. In these letters, you don't write anything that you don't want people to remember about you in the future.

Thirdly, it is helpful in encouraging the writer to improve their writing skills, which could one day be a benefit.

When I was courting, this method of communication was incredibly beneficial. At the time, there were fewer people using telephones, and we both lived in different cities. We have personally benefited from some of the benefits of letter-writing communication that are mentioned above. We still refer to some of those letters even today, after all these years. My husband recently read a passage from one of those letters that was written twenty years ago at a church service. While he was preaching, it greatly assisted in bringing home several points. What if they weren't in the shape of letters? Having them as resources would not have been possible! Having Fun With Mutual Interests Although these are very important, courtship is not merely a time for prayer, fasting, and studying the Bible. Additionally, it is a moment for people to bond through shared interests. You two might both like taking pictures, for instance. why not Enjoy yourself, but stay away from sin. Such images can be stored for later use as references. I recently came upon these photos of my husband and I from around 27 years ago, before we got hitched. It was really enjoyable! Those moments aid in determining whether you two are truly destined to be together or not.

Maintain Your Purity!

Flee also young lusts; rather, pursue righteousness, faith, charity, and peace with those who pray to the Lord with sincerity. 22 Timothy 2

All marriages are honorable, and the bed is pure; yet, God will judge whoremongers and adulterers. -Heb.13:4

This warning is required at this point because, when you love someone and spend time with them, you are inevitably drawn to want to touch, feel, caress, and cuddle them. If caution is not exercised, one "small" thing will inevitably result in many, until the bed is dirty. I've seen a lot of families struggle because of this.

In this region of the world, there is a proverb that goes, "If you're going to eat soup all day, why rush out of it in the morning?" I can only be as literal as that.

Wait if you're courting, is my advise to you. Be tolerant. Your moment is near. You must cease messing yourself up and defiling the marriage bed immediately to prevent your destiny from being thwarted. Anyone who intentionally defiles the marriage bed is depriving themselves of the honor of marriage (Hebrews 13:4).

In case you missed it, if you truly repent, God will pardon you and give you back your marriage honor. However, you must not return to your vomit and must instead abstain from such behavior.

The Crucial Next Step on the Road to Marriage

A Specified Engagement

A moment must be set out to formally and publicly present yourself to your parents, relatives, and friends in order to satisfy all righteousness. It is also a time for dowry payments in some cultures.

Don't just pick up a woman and leave to begin life as husband and wife. This is especially inappropriate for a Christian. Wisdom recommends that you attend a formal engagement in order to honor the family of your future wife or spouse. Pay the dowry as required, but make sure that nothing you do goes against your Christian principles. You must only give dowries that will exalt God and not offend your conscience.

I focused my attention on Isaac and Rebekah's wedding. Even though it is not a normal wedding because Isaac did not personally seek out Rebekah, we may still draw some lessons from it. We can see that Rebekah's people were only given valuable and honorable items, not objects for rituals, in Genesis 24:53 " And the servant brought out precious items for Rebekah, including clothing, silver and gold jewelry, and precious items for her mother and brother as well." It is highly scriptural to pay dowry, let me say that out loud. It is wise to follow this procedure.

U-turns are allowed!

Some people rush into being married that they don't take the time to get to know one another or won't be honest with one another. The courtship stage is when you can demonstrate everything about your partner. You have made the decision to spend the rest of your lives together, but you must also be careful not to take anything for granted. My husband frequently quips that frustration is born out of assumption.

You must not give up on your trip in disappointment.

"Prove everything; cling to what is right." 5:21 in 1 Thessalonians

A U-turn is allowed if you two find out through romance that you cannot "walk" together, that is, that you are incompatible and hence cannot make it together. a turnabout in the sense of ending the courtship. End the relationship if you think you made the incorrect decision! If necessary, a broken courtship is acceptable. Breaking up with a courtship is preferable to divorcing your spouse. A failed courtship is not the same as a divorce, after all!

A Christian Wedding in Public

Every successful courtship ought to end in wedlock. On a horizontal level, marriage is a covenant between a man and a woman, and on a vertical level, it is a covenant between God and both of them. It is crucial to have a public Christian wedding ceremony in a church that upholds the Bible for this reason.

You formally invite God to be the third party in your union when you get married in a church.

A triple cord is not easily broken, according to Ecclesiastes 4:12: "And if one succeed against him, two shall withstand him."

In light of this, you shouldn't simply pick up a woman, go beneath a tree, ask a friend to officiate and bless the union, and then you're done! No! The worst-case scenario is that you just decide to move in together casually. One of the main causes of marriages dissolving after a few years is the absence of a true Christian wedding. Although a public wedding gives your family, friends, and well-wishers from near and far the chance to experience the joy of the day with you, marriage is a covenant partnership between two people.

People cannot deny knowing you are married if you have a Christian wedding in public. Although some young women and even some men don't mind dating married men or women in this "fast" age, a public wedding helps keep them off! It makes your surroundings sterile. What else? It has been found that marriages performed in a church have a higher success rate than marriages performed elsewhere.

FIXING MISSPUN ACTIONS

People who have been living together with their partners without paying the dowry, having a formal engagement, or having a public Christian wedding may find these materials upsetting. Why not do things right rather than feeling or living in condemnation? Get moving straight now, and go pay the dowry! If you fit this description but are not legally married, you should "legalize" your relationship. You can accomplish this, for example, by attending a court wedding. Then seek out a gospel minister to bless your union.

A mistake is never undone by time! If an error was made yesterday, it is still wrong today. You can rectify wrongs! Because they abhor this successful path, many people endure unnecessary suffering. Because their union was "illegal," I have witnessed women being ruthlessly expelled from their houses after their spouses passed away. As she has no legal standing, the woman has no voice. Directing wisdom is profitable!

Parents Beware!

I have to issue a warning to the Christian parents present. Please allow your kids the freedom to make their own decisions and take responsibility for them. They can only reach adulthood in this way. They will groan if you do not allow them to expand! Do not urge that they wed members of a specific tribe or someone who works in a specific field. Allow them to follow God's leading in their lives about marriage as long as the man or woman is of their choosing, is born-again, and satisfies all the other requirements covered in this chapter. You share in it when everything is going well for them. In the name of Jesus, all will go well for you!

CHAPTER 5

YOUR COMMUNICATIONS STRATEGY SHOULD BE AMPLIFIE

We talked about the family in the previous chapters in relation to God's blueprint or overall plan for it. We have also learned why God values strong families, what a home's foundation should look like, and how to lay a good one.

But if you stopped there, it would be like many construction projects that were abandoned in the middle. Because of this, after establishing a strong foundation, we must talk about the many components needed to create a happy family.

For every house was constructed by a human being, but God is the true creator of everything. (Hebrews 3:4)

Building a real house is labor-intensive effort! A wonderful home cannot be dreamt into existence; it is the result of hard work. In addition to all the other intricate details that go into its creation, blocks must be placed strategically one on top of the other. A lot of effort, resources, and knowledge are required.

Like a physical building, families must put in a lot of effort to become magnificent. If it is to succeed, each member must intentionally give their fair share. There is no successful family that falls from heaven, just as no real house falls from the sky; rather, every successful family you see was "made".

Although prayer is crucial for a home's success, it is insufficient on its own. A couple can pray for a happy household from now till tomorrow on their knees. If they don't figure out what they have to do to succeed and put effort into it, it will all be for nothing.

Building a quality house requires thought and planning.

A successful marriage and family are dependent on having

effective communication. It is vital to continually hone your communication techniques and tactics.

Regardless of how well you now interact with your spouse and family members, there is always room for improvement. Anything you do can always be done more effectively. According to a statement made by someone, there is always space for development. Never assume that your communications are being received in the greatest way possible. If you want to constantly improve your communication techniques, you can communicate more effectively than you are now. We'll be thinking about how in this section.

Why Is Communication Required?

Effective communication is the cornerstone of any family relationship that wants to last. The absence of this is what is causing so much tension in many homes. It could be said to be the "mortar" that binds a marriage together. The secret to a happy marriage is communication. If you talk together, you stay together, as a wise man once said, and I firmly believe this to be true. And you are aware that a marriage involves living together! It will be easier for you to understand the value of effective communication if we take a closer look at the first family, Adam's family. The tree of the knowledge of good and evil was forbidden to Adam by God. I suppose Adam understood the importance of this command, but he failed to convey it to Eve in a convincing manner. I suppose she treated it lightly. If you carefully read the account, you will notice that during Eve's conversation with the serpent, she used the word "said" rather than "commanded." God, however, did not just say it; He also commanded it!

But you must not eat from the tree of the knowledge of good and evil because you will undoubtedly die the day you do. (Genesis 2:17)

We want to draw attention to the word "commanded." Actually, the word's meaning is "order...authoritative instruction that something be done." A command is unarguable and nonnegotiable. The first family's mistake was Adam's failure to explain the gravity of the situation to his wife over a meal. (This is not to say that Eve was faultless in every way. She should have told the serpent to hold off until Adam got home if she wasn't sure what to say to it.

The problem is that Adam ought to have taken the initiative in this situation as well. Today, a lot of families are in trouble because the men (husbands) who should be taking the initiative in matters affecting their families don't! This, in my opinion, is one of my own family's strengths. My husband, for instance, has been a great help to me in understanding the vision God has given him and the various stages it is going through. I then impart those guidelines to our kids so that there is never a breakdown in communication at any level.

You must be persuaded of one thing: marriage is about sharing lives together; it is an association between two people who have given their lives to God first and to one another later. Therefore, the man and his wife must speak to each other alone before discussing other family members. God cannot take over that obligation. He won't travel from heaven to your house to intervene in your wife's or kids' matters. This obligation cannot be transferred!

A SUCCESSFUL COMMUNICATION

Poor communication is a common cause of divorce. Understanding what communication is and the components that improve it are prerequisites for good communication.

What is communication?

Simply put, communication is the skill of having meaningful conversations. It is intended to be stimulating and two-sided. It is intended to be a forum for expressing emotions and working out disagreements in the family, maintaining the stability of your relationship. According to the dictionary, it is "the technique of transmitting information through; the transmission of concepts." Two-Way Dialog Effective communication requires two-way interaction. Before it can be deemed communication, the husband and wife must both take part in dialogues. If the communication is one-sided, it is not a dialogue. A marriage is strengthened by open communication, which forges an unbreakable link.

Talk to express who you are! Some people are unable to express their true feelings to anyone. This shouldn't be happening in a familial relationship. Learn to express your thoughts, emotions, joys, anxieties, challenges, and plans. Discuss them with the person you love!

You'll find that as you accomplish that, your link will deepen and your partnership will be firmly established. In turn, this will promote harmony and respect for one another. It turns into a time of wonderful communion after everyone has access to one another.

It All Begins With God

You must improve your relationship with God in order to have open communication with your spouse and other family members. Hebrews 3:4's verse explains that even if someone built each house, God is ultimately the one who is in charge of construction.

The family is ultimately built by God. Because of this, communication within families suffers when a man or woman lacks efficient contact with God. As a result, your marriage will suffer as a result. Therefore, keep the channels of communication open between you and God at all times. Learn to exchange ideas with Him so that His great mind can sharpen your small one. The next query is, "How do I properly interact with God?"

Thanksgiving, praise, and worship

The most important way is to live a life of thanksgiving, adoration, and worship. If you are a "Godpraiser," your relationship with your spouse and family will suffer as a result. You will develop your gratitude, courtesy, consideration, and loyalty. You will have the ability to live in peace with God and others by "...teaching and admonishing one another in psalms and hymns and spiritual melodies, singing with grace in our hearts to the Lord." Colossians 3:16

Praise will naturally flow from an attitude of grace in the heart. Learn to praise God for what He has done in your life, thank Him for what He will accomplish, and worship Him for who He is! You won't have anything to gripe or grumble about once you do this. Then there will never be a reason to accuse God. Who will defend you if you charge God?

Ingratitude is demonstrated by accusations, muttering, and moaning. Nothing paralyzes a discourse like accusations, muttering, and whining! Get away from it. It is so grave that the Bible warns against murmuring, "Neither murmur ye, as some of them also muttered, and were killed of the destroyer." 1 Corinthians 10:10

"And when the people grumbled, the Lord was offended; and when the Lord heard it, he was enraged; and the fire of the LORD burned among them, and devoured them who were in the farthest parts of the camp." Numbers 11:1

You whine, murmur, and grumble because you believe God hasn't treated you fairly. Keep in mind that God is always right! He is constantly working for your benefit and for the best interests of you.

You can communicate with men if you know how to do so with God. The key is to have an attitude of gratitude!

Living a Life of Prayer

Another important approach to communicate with God is through a life of prayer. Simply put, prayer is communication with God. It is a two-way, intentional interaction between you and God.

Lord, teach us to pray, the apostles prayed to Jesus in Luke 11:1.

Therefore, teaching about prayer is necessary. It's important to impart the art of prayer to people. Be cautious about nothing, but in everything, make requests known to God in prayer and petition with thanksgiving, according to Philippians 4:6.

This demonstrates unequivocally that you can communicate your wishes to God through prayer and receive their responses. What a privilege!

You know that you were Gentiles, dragged away to these stupid idols, even as you were led, the Bible says in 1 Corinthians 12 verse 2 while discussing spiritual gifts.

A false god is an idol. It is something that is obviously there but has no real substance. Idols have dumb minds as one of their traits. But halleluiah, our God is not a moron! God speaks! God converses with you when you speak with Him. a God who speaks, comparable to speaking people!

Your approach to communicating with guys will be significantly improved if you learn how to commune with God. A fruitful communion with God is the foundation for a fruitful conversation with your spouse in particular and your family in general. Never forget that if you can communicate with God, you can communicate with men as well.

Different Forms of Communication

There are two types of communication: verbal and nonverbal. When there are words involved, it is verbal. The utilization of actions, facial expressions, body language, letters, etc. are all examples of nonverbal communication.

One of the keys to marital and family success is mastering the art of verbal communication. Never think negatively about your wife or husband before going to bed. You can get nightmares and unpleasant dreams if you do! Make sure that everything that has to be addressed is done on the same day. The bond between you and your spouse, as well as between you and your family members, will be "cemented" in large part by this. Explosions are unavoidable if complaints are not voiced. It makes me think of what can happen to a Coca-Cola bottle if it is shaken frequently over time. Eventually, it will explode, smashing the bottle. Therefore, it becomes crucial for families and couples to make sure that nothing that cannot be resolved interferes with their relationship.

"Be furious, but do not transgress; do not let the sun set on your rage; do not give the devil a foothold." -Eph. 4:26–27

Your partner won't ignore or berate you if what you have to say is important and pertinent to him. Never let a conversation turn into a heated argument. If you do, you are letting the devil in. Many people prioritize winning arguments over winning their partners. Beware of arguments that drive you further apart from one another!

For instance, as a woman, you could not concur with a choice your spouse makes. The best course of action at that point is to listen to him express his viewpoint and, after he is done, to express your own viewpoint as well. Suspend the conversation until a later time if, for any reason, you feel that an argument is going to break out. In your prayers, express your thoughts to your heavenly father and ask for the appropriate words, appropriate moment, and appropriate tactic. However, never argue!

"Whoever handles a situation carefully will come out well; and blessed is he who trusts in the LORD." in Proverbs 16:20

If every conversation you have ends in an argument, a gully is being formed between you both, and if it is not addressed right away, it could cause complete separation.

At this point, it is vital to point out that some people speak carelessly in an effort to express themselves. Indiscretion is lacking in this. Words are as delicate as raw eggs; once cracked, they cannot be reassembled, therefore consider your words carefully before speaking.

"Do not let any corrupt communication come out of your mouth, but only that which is useful for edifying, that it may impart grace to those listening." – Ephesians 4:29

Some males, especially when angry, call their spouses and kids the worst names possible. In turn, some women are skilled nags. That verbal harassment is unacceptable! The tongue is intended to be a tool for edification; God did not make it to speak bad words. It is impossible for sweet and bitter water to come from the same source at the same time (Jms 3:11).

Many people abuse their tongues since they don't know what it's for.

Death and life are determined by the power of the tongue, and those who love it will consume its fruit. 18:21 in Proverbs

"With the words of thy mouth, thou art taken, art snared with the words of thy tongue." – Proverbs 6:2.

Because the tongue is not being controlled, there are houses that are severely damaged and in difficulties. These homes are the victims of dishonest speech. However, Ephesians 4:29 places the burden of proof on us. No corrupt communication should ever leave your mouth, it warns. You must watch what you say since you are responsible for it. Recently, a woman gave the following moving testimony:

Poor communication can make a marriage fail for a pair. You must have faith in God for him to place hot coals on your tongue. No husband likes a nagging wife. In a similar way, no woman wants a whiny husband. It's time to stop bugging people, or you'll get stopped eventually.

Gossip is another example of bad communication. You must avoid gossip as a family. Never be caught criticizing and backbiting other family members while they are away. It causes hostility and division within a family.

The use of words is crucial in communicating. The development of communication technology has shrunk the once vast world we live in. However, poor communication is a common cause of divorce. You must learn how to pick the proper words to say things in order to consistently enhance your verbal communication technique and abilities. In other words, the proper words will produce the right atmosphere, while the wrong words will produce the wrong atmosphere. Correct language, the means of effective communication, is the foundation of healthy relationships.

The use of conversational tools other than words is known as non-verbal communication. This category includes words, gestures, body language, and actions. That makes me think of the proverb, "Your deed speaks louder than your voice,"

You have to realize that your expression is more significant than anything else you wear. For instance, there is a way to convey your displeasure without speaking. You can tell when your husband is furious, unhappy, excited, etc. just by looking at his body language.

The longer you live with someone, the better you become at interpreting their body language. For instance, a glance from your husband can convey to you a message that no one else may be able to interpret. That is communicating nonverbally.

As I wrap off this section, let me reiterate that communication is important for all family members, not just spouses and wives. In order for a family relationship to be successful, members must use both verbal and nonverbal forms of communication. Maintain open channels of communication and prevent the enemy from interfering.

Keeping the Lines of Communication Open

The first step when requesting a telephone line for your home is to visit the appropriate organization and submit an application. A phone number is given to you after you are requested to buy a box that allows you to receive and make calls. If you meet the prerequisites, you are free to pick up your receiver once you are connected and call any number of your choosing. However, you can only call other linked parties! Not only that. Before there can be a meaningful conversation on the phone, the other party must answer the call. I wish to link this idea to how a husband and wife and other family members communicate in the following few pages.

Talking and Listening

Communication is a two-way process that involves talking and listening. Husband and wife should make a habit of talking about matters that matter to them. This will involve time, but such time spent is never a waste, but an investment. It is not so much of how long, but how well. Such times help in developing personal relationship with each other, which in turn brings about harmony.

"A good communicator is always a good listener." In essence, a good communicator is not one who talks all the time, but one who knows when to talk and when to listen. There is a time for everything, says the Preacher in Ecclesiastes 3:1.

Can you imagine how frustrating it will be for you to receive a phone call from a friend who spends twenty minutes talking, never allowing you to say a word? You may listen politely the first time, but certainly not the next time. When next he or she calls, you will definitely not be keen to pick up the phone.

For communication to be meaningful, when one person is talking, the other should listen. See what God's word says in James 1:19: "Wherefore, my beloved brethren, let every man be swift to hear, slow to speak, slow to wrath."

This means that you should listen more than you talk! Someone has said that this is the reason why God gave man two ears, but only one mouth!

One person should not be the only one talking throughout. No matter your temperament, never monopolize a discussion; give room to your spouse or other family members present as well.

If your partner is an introvert, and you are an extrovert, be patient enough to allow him time to talk and wait for him to finish before you respond. This requires discipline, however. Good lovers are usually good listeners! Learn to listen.

The same principle works when you are handling difficulties or resolving differences. Both of you should speak in turns; one at a time. You should allow your spouse to finish speaking before you talk. Both of you should not be found talking at the same time; before you know it you will be pointing at each other, and the one with larger muscles begins to warm up for a final show down.

God is a God of order, and every thing ought to be done decently and in order!

The Place of Understanding

"Good understanding giveth favour: but the way of transgressors is hard." -Proverbs 13:15

"Through wisdom is an house builded; and by understanding it is established." Proverbs 24:3

These scriptures reveal the vital place of understanding in establishing a successful family. To establish means to "set up on a permanent basis, to make secure or permanent in a certain place". This means that peace, joy, love, and favour can be set up on a permanent basis in your family. It also means you can secure or make your relationship with your household permanent by possessing good understanding.

When you possess good understanding, you will correctly interpret what your spouse or family members say, rather than read negative meanings to every statement and action. Understanding helps you read between the lines.

Relating this to the natural, when you receive a call from someone, until you understand what that person is saying, he cannot be said to have communicated. So it goes beyond talking to understanding, having a clear picture, or what the dictionary defines as to "know and comprehend the nature or meaning of something, realize or grasp (something)". Therefore, understanding is a crucial aspect of communication.

Give Room For Possible Questions

Any seasoned communicator knows that in order to ascertain how effective he has been in passing across a piece of information, he needs a response from his audience. The response can come by way of comments, contributions or questions.

A question is an expression of inquiry that invites or calls for a reply. Relevant questions, when asked, shed light on the subject in question. The reason there is a lot of misunderstanding in some homes (which in most cases results into quarrels), is assumption. Your spouse has said something, you clearly don't understand, and instead of asking for clarification, you assume she means one thing, when actually she means an entirely different thing.

"Assumption is the mother of frustration." That means, to assume you understand when you actually did not invariably leads to frustration. That is one reason so many people are terribly frustrated in their marriage and family life. Personally, I don't assume I understand a thing. When I am in doubt on an issue, I look for an opportunity to ask relevant questions. There is no crime in asking questions to improve your understanding of a subject matter. If you must not become a question mark, learn to ask questions!

Remember the account between Philip and the Ethiopian eunuch in Acts chapter 8? Read the following verses: "...Understandest thou what thou readest? And he said, how can I, except some man should guide me?... And the eunuch answered Philip, and said, I pray thee, of whom speaketh the prophet this? Of himself, or of some other man? Then Philip opened his mouth, and from the same scripture, and preached unto him Jesus." -Acts 8:30-35

Asking relevant questions brought complete transformation for the Ethiopian eunuch, as well as fulfillment of ministry to Philip. Questions are an integral part of communication, if it is going to be meaningful.

As a man, don't just "issue" instructions without giving your wife or children room to ask questions if they have one, or seek clarification. Don't ignore them or shout at them; rather, help their understanding. Spend time to explain until they understand. If Adam had done this, I suppose he would have saved himself and his family a lot of trouble.

The importance of proper timing.

Communication requires precise timing. Knowing "when" to say "what," in other words. Consider a woman whose exhausted husband has just arrived home from work. She welcomes him and tells him there is nothing in the house, so he shouldn't anticipate any meals. And you ponder why he becomes so enraged! Never forget the saying, "A man is what he eats"!

Although it might be true that there is no food in the house, it was spoken in the incorrect context, at the incorrect moment, and in the incorrect location. Knowing "when" to communicate "what" is crucial. Saying things at random times is unwise.

A fool says whatever is on his mind, but a wise man holds it back till after. 29:11 in Proverbs

Although the knowledgeable understands when and where to say it, he nevertheless expresses what is on his mind. Find the appropriate location and time to address any issues you have. Not in front of your spouse's coworkers, not when he or she is hungry or exhausted.

Your method of expressing a problem is crucial. Additionally, even if your strategy may be sound, your tone of voice could be discouraging. Saying the right thing at the wrong time, in the wrong place, or with the wrong voice tone frequently causes conflict in families.

"A man has joy in his answer; and how good is a word given in proper season?" in Proverbs 15:23

Every word has its "proper season"! However, knowing when something is due requires wisdom.

The Bible mentions the 10 virgins who awaited the bridegroom in Matthew 25. The other five were described as wise, while five were called foolish. I understood that timing was what distinguished them from one another. The ignorant did what the smart ones did, but at the wrong time. Time is everything.

The Need For Good Intentions

The goal of the commandment is generosity that comes from a pure heart, a clear conscience, and genuine faith. Timotheus 1:5

God looks beyond what you say to your intent when you say something. Although your spouse and family can hear what you say, they might not understand why you said it. The Bible mentions a pure conscience because of this. Make sure that whatever you say comes from a place of pure consciousness.

Don't be like some men who ask their spouses to repeat what they said to them at 10:00 a.m. yesterday when they phone them late at night. Now tell me. Why are you unsure? What do you mean you forgot? He then hits the wife as she is trying to gather her thoughts. Do not laugh; it occurs! The man's only intention is to remark, "I warned you not to leave this cup here. How come you did it? He decides to complicate matters for her rather than take a straightforward approach.

God is aware of the reasons behind your actions. Nothing is hidden from His all-seeing eyes, not even your innermost thoughts:

It is important to observe this strong verse from Proverbs 15:3 in this context. "The Lord's eyes are everywhere, looking at both good and evil."

This has served as my life's compass. It has greatly aided me in making sure that God will accept my motives in everything I do. My prayer for you is that you will make an effort, by God's grace, to assure motive purity in all of your contact, especially with your family members, starting right now.

The Benefits of Communication

Effective communication has benefits. They consist of the following, but are not restricted to: In any household with good communication, intimacy is always there. Here, intimacy refers to proximity. This is due to the fact that the closer you become as you learn to communicate, the harder it will be for the devil to enter into your relationship. Because they stick together, the husband and wife continue to be together.

Another benefit of efficient communication is friendship. The foundation of friendship is emotional attachment and familiarity. You get to know one another better the more you talk to one another. You become emotionally attached to each other as a result of this. Love is inextricably linked to emotion. It is emotional attachment that causes you to develop feelings for one another. According to my husband, danger approaches when a husband and wife quit feeling affection for one another.

Self-awareness is a benefit of effective communication as well. This aids in improving your self-awareness. Your partner and family members act as human mirrors to help you identify the "stains on your back" and help you become a better version of yourself. Your spouse, children, and/or other loved ones can help you better understand who you are when the channels of communication are open. As a result, you are able to identify and address defects in your life and character that you previously may not have been aware of. As a result, acceptance results.

Effective communication also encourages love and submission, which is another benefit. It encourages the husband to love and the wife to submit. When a woman disobeys her husband's orders, it's not always because she's rebelling or trying to be difficult; sometimes it's because she doesn't understand.

Love is sparked when communication tactics are continually refined. When a husband and wife are in good communication, it is simpler for him to shower her with affection, and she finds it easier to submit to him without feeling forced.

A man's inability to love his wife is an indication of his poor relationship with her. However, when the channels of communication are open, rather than harboring resentments, both of them can freely address problems and come to advantageous solutions.

I can personally attest that submitting to my husband in everything is a joy for me! I do so easily and voluntarily; he doesn't need to force me. Not because of his titles, but rather because of the open channels of contact. Effective communication keeps enticing him to love me and me to submit to him. He then turns to me with assurance and says, "I just love you."

It's okay for kids to ask their parents any questions they may have. To prevent them from being wayward, kids should feel cherished. In an environment where there is free communication between parents and children, children readily and naturally obey their parents. Because they comprehend their parents' commands so well, disobedience does not flourish in the household. Because we are always looking for ways to improve communication in our home, our children naturally behave in ways that have a positive impact on the work because they have a clear grasp of God's plan for our family. Despite having a busy schedule as king of Israel, King David found time to speak with his son, Solomon. Every time they spoke, he would laud the merits of wisdom. Solomon records one such incident in Proverbs 4:3–9. All people, especially fathers, can benefit greatly from understanding this lesson.

Because I was my father's son and my mother's only tenderly regarded child, He instructed me as well and advised me to obey his commands in order to live, saying, "Let thy heart retain my words. Get understanding and wisdom; do not disregard this advice or back away from it. Love her, and she will keep you; don't abandon her, and she will protect you. Gain wisdom since it is the most important thing, and with everything you have, get insight. When you elevate her, she will advance you; when you embrace her, she will elevate you. She will bestow a grace-filled ornament on thy head and grant thee a crown of glory. It's understandable why this story appears in 1 Kings 3:5–13. "At a dream when Solomon was in Gibeon, the LORD appeared to him and said, "Ask what I shall grant thee. And Solomon remarked, "Now, LORD my God, you have appointed thy servant to rule in place of David my father." Therefore, grant your servant an understanding heart so that I may evaluate your people and distinguish between good and wicked. For who is able to judge this great a nation of yours? And Solomon's speech, in which he made this request, delighted the Lord. And God replied, "Because you asked this, and have not asked riches for yourself, nor have you asked for the life of your enemies, but have asked for understanding to discern judgment, behold, I have done according to your words: lo, I have given thee a wise and an understanding heart; so that none like thee was before thee, nor shall any arise after thee." There won't be another monarch like you for the rest of your days because I gave you both the riches and the honor you did not ask for.

What a wonderful benefit of clear and successful communication! Fathers, develop communication skills with your kids and instill in them the values that will help them succeed in life. Help them understand the value of the key things in life by communicating with them. Because parents haven't taught their kids morally upright ideals, there are so many criminals and robbers today.

Another example is found in Proverbs 31:1–5, which reads: "The prophecy his mother taught him, the words of King Lemuel. My son, what? And what, the child I conceived? And who are you, my vows' son? Do not lend your strength to women or your ways to that which overthrows kings. Wine and strong drinks are not appropriate for kings, O Lemuel, nor are either for princes, lest they forget the law and erroneously judge one of the oppressed.

A child that grows up with this kind of admonition will not wander away from the path of righteousness. So parents rise up and take your place.

The gains of communication cannot be over emphasized. Open lines of communication between family members can lead to the preservation of lives and destinies. Look at this: it was Abigail's openness that delivered her entire household from the wrath of King David, provoked by the foolishness of Nabal. The communication line was so open that a steward could approach the "Madam" of the house to give her valuable information that eventually brought deliverance to her household (I Sam. 25:14). (I Sam. 25:14).

In conclusion, let me reiterate that constant improvement on your communication strategy is vital for a successful family. You can't do without it!

CHAPTER 6

BE DETERMINED

Any successful relationship, including marriage and the family, is built on commitment. It acts as the glue holding a marriage together. The likelihood of a family surviving when there is a lack of commitment between a husband and wife is quite low. Commitment is to marriage and family what the spinal cord is to the human body. The body will be limp and paralyzed without it.

Due to a lack of dedication, families with high achievement potential experience tremendous setbacks and failure. I once heard about a 25-year marriage that ended in divorce because both the husband and woman lacked commitment.

You must be dedicated to the institution of marriage as well as to your spouse if you want your family to succeed. "What therefore God hath joined together, let not man pull asunder," says this magnificent verse. -Mark 10:9

God has brought you together, but you still need to remain dedicated to one another so that nothing can tear you apart. The Bible again states that a man must leave his father and mother and cling to his wife because they will become one flesh in Genesis 2:24.

In essence, God is stating that a man must abandon his parents and dedicate himself to both his wife and the institution of marriage; as a result, they become one flesh. And the wife is the same. How devoted are you to your marriage and family, husband and wife? Commitment is necessary if you want to enjoy success as a family.

Describe commitment.

"An engagement or responsibility that restricts freedom of action" is what a commitment is. In other words, because of your commitment, there are some things you cannot do. In 1 Corinthians 6:12, the apostle Paul stated, "All things are legal unto me, but all things are not expedient."

You pick the expedient above the right thing out of loyalty. You are forced to give up some of the things you enjoy or find enjoyable. In the best interests of the family, it may occasionally be necessary to give up rights and privileges that are rightfully yours.

two tiers of commitment

Both God and man (your spouse) are subject to commitment. The first comes first. The first is the cornerstone of the second. Hebrews 3:4 shows that although every house is created by a man, God is ultimately the one who constructs everything. That means all of your building efforts are useless without God. This reality is reiterated in John 15:5. For without me, you are powerless.

dedication to God

If you can demonstrate a man's sincere devotion to the Lord, I can demonstrate a man's dedication to the welfare of his family. They complement each other. Anyone who has made a commitment to God will naturally make a commitment to their spouse as well.

If I agreed with the contents, he then asked me to sign. I could see his devotion to God and His kingdom, and because I shared that devotion, I was certain that we were traveling in the same path. That's why I don't think I have the right to argue with God or even ask "Why?" now, wherever God wants my husband to go. I registered for it years ago. I don't remark, "Oh, what about my pals," as we leave a city. God is superior to all other beings!

We are so devoted to God that I wouldn't feel bad if we missed a church service. The words "we are giving an offering of so many millions to God" are whispered in my ear by my husband. This is a result of the whole commitment to God I made in 1976.

When I was a nursing mother, I once came home with my full paycheck and bent down to give it to my husband. God talked to me before you arrived and told me that we should treat everything like a seed, he added. The fact that vital supplies were being rationed at the time and were scarce in Nigeria added to the difficulty of the situation. Then, despite having money, one might not be able to buy the necessary goods. But what occurs if there is absolutely no money? But for us, the all-sufficient God was more than enough! After investing my entire paycheck, we were no longer in need since, because to God's extraordinary provisions, we were able to distribute to individuals in our neighborhood.

God established matrimony. The institution of marriage is greater than the individuals who participate in it. Therefore, dedication to the institution of marriage rather than merely to the individuals in it is the key to creating a successful marriage and family.

Marriage is dignified and honorable. Sometimes, the people who make up it might not be. Although God created marriage as a perfect institution, people are not flawless. Marriage remains the same throughout a person's lifetime. It's a steadfast institution. Therefore, those involved in a marriage must learn to respect marriage itself in order to create a good one. The trick is in this!

Before you agree to wed anyone, young lady or guy, find out how devoted he or she is to God and to marriage. How committed he or she will be to your marriage will depend on how committed he or she is to God. You might be wondering why your husband isn't committed to your marriage because you married a man who wasn't committed to God. Because of the weak foundation, he is unable to. First, he must "sell out" to God!

There is still some hope, though. God is able to replace your problems with peace, your grief with joy, and your breakdowns with breakthroughs. Just like He did in Mark 4:37–39 when He calmed the storm and the boat's rocking stopped, He can stabilize the rocking in your home. Put what you are learning in this book to use to give God a chance. If you let Him, our God will offer you a fresh start and deliver you from oppression!

Commitment to Your Spouse

A successful marriage also requires commitment to your spouse. Without this, no amount of prayer, fasting, and "sleeping" in church can prevent your home from falling apart. Nothing can take the place of commitment in the building of a successful marriage. Marriage is not a temporary arrangement, but a commitment for life. If this is true, you may wonder why the divorce rate is so high, even among Christians. The reason is that many people are not committed to each other. Commitment is the framework on which a marriage is built. A man and his wife must, therefore, be totally committed to each other spiritually, physically, emotionally and otherwise. Commitment in turn brings security. A successful marriage must be exclusive, involving no other. One man and one woman, in one life-time relationship. Each spouse must commit to "forsake all others". For example, a woman must be so committed to her husband that no amount of money any other man offers her to have illicit sex with her will be strong enough to make her give it a second thought. So also, a man must be so committed to his wife that if his wife and mother were both in a state of emergency and needed rescue, he will naturally rescue his wife first before his mother.

The two levels of commitment we have discussed above can be compared to the hob of a bicycle, which holds all the spokes of the wheel together. However, no matter how effective the spokes may be, without the hob, the bicycle is going nowhere. Therefore, without commitment, no matter what else is in place, that family is going nowhere.

Commitment Compels Love

"Husbands, love your wives, even as Christ also loved the church, and gave himself for it." -Ephesians 5:25

A husband's primary responsibility is that of loving his wife, and Commitment compels love. That is, where there is commitment to God and to one's spouse, love becomes automatic. Commitment becomes like a driving force, pushing the husband to love his wife. When I see a man who finds it difficult to love his wife, I know that the problem is essentially that of lack of commitment to God and to his marriage. When there is commitment, there will be no need to persuade a man to love his wife; it will come naturally. My husband, for instance, is highly committed to God and to the success of our home, therefore, it is easy for him to ravish me with so much love, even without my asking for it. That is commitment! Husbands, you need to hear this. There is no wife who hates to be loved. There is no woman that will not respond positively to love. Someone once said that submission is a response, because when you love your wife she responds by submitting. Therefore, tension and quarreling in a home is an indication of the absence of love. The same principle goes for other members of the family. Commitment to the success of your family makes a man invest time into the lives of his children. He ensures the children have a constant assurance of his love.

Give Voice To Your Commitment

A commitment to love your family is not complete until you give voice to it. Men can never understand what these three simple words, "I love you" can do to a woman. Surprisingly, some men find it difficult to give voice to their commitment. A man testified during one of our annual conventions that for a long time he had found it extremely difficult to give voice to his commitment by expressing his love to his wife. He obeyed the instruction to do so, and things began to change positively in his home. Expressing love to your legitimate wife or children should not be a difficult thing to do! For some who think it is an unrighteous thing to do, was Jesus unrighteous? Thrice He asked Peter if he loved Him. Remember that Jesus was never married, but His disciples represented His earthly wife in a figure. So in essence,

He was saying to His "wife", "I love you; do you love Me?" Don't read this book without putting the contents to work. Husbands, if you have not been giving voice to your commitment, it is time to get started. And if you already have, there is still room for improvement. Learn to look straight into her eyes and tell her how much you love her, and you will see the change in her countenance. No matter how spiritual a woman is, she still wants to be told that she is loved. I can tell you this as a woman I want to hear my husband give voice to his commitment by telling me how much he loves me, and he does! These are some of the things that hold our home together. I must say a word concerning children here. Children like to be touched and cuddled. A touch communicates warmth. Hug them, kiss them; let them feel a sense of being connected with you by your warm embraces. It is not unrighteous. It is a mortar bonding you together. It keeps the assurance of your love burning at times when words are clumsy.

Commitment Triggers Submission

Just as commitment provokes love, it also triggers submission. Any woman who is truly committed to the success of her marriage will be submissive to her husband. When a woman is stubborn and naughty, it is a sign of lack of commitment to her home. What is submission? Simply defined, it means willingly putting yourself under someone else's authority. Contrary to some people's thinking, submission has nothing to do with slavery. Rather, it is an act of the will. A committed woman needs no advice to submit to her husband. Her commitment is a driving force. I am not talking about submission under duress, but from a willing heart. Many people wish and express their desire that their home be like ours, but as the saying goes, "If wishes were horses beggars will ride." Nothing good happens by chance. Commitment must be in place, else family success will be a mere dream. Thank God for His grace, but we have been committed to playing our parts too. That is why today I can boldly declare that I am enjoying a good home! As you play your part also, God will give you a brighter testimony than ours! Wherever there is commitment in a marriage, there will be love and submission: both parties working together for the success of their home. Personally, I don't find it stressful to submit to my husband. Not just now, but right from the days of little beginnings. I never had to be coerced into doing so. I always have found it a thing of great joy. Single ladies, before you get into a marriage relationship with any man, ensure that you can submit to him without duress. If you find it difficult to submit to him during courtship, then don't marry him! This is because you will not submit to him in marriage, and that is signing in for trouble. An area where many women find it difficult to submit in marriage is in their finances. Money is a "god" to such women. They may submit to the man in other areas, but when it comes to finances, forget it! I learnt to submit my earnings to my husband right from the time I was engaged in secular employment. Mark you, I was not just throwing it at him, but handing it over to him respectfully. That's why now he does not wait for me to ask for money; he just keeps giving to me! I would, however, like to sound a note of caution here, for the sake of balance. It was easy for me to hand over my salary to my husband because our relationship permitted that. I could trust him. He was not bullying me or spending the money in an unaccountable manner. Men, if you want to enjoy this type of co-operation from your wife, make sure you build a relationship with her that will permit that. Don't expect your wife to hand over her earnings to you if you treat her with disrespect, or if you are uncommunicative and unaccountable in your spending habits. Don't expect her to submit all her income to you if you are going to spend it frivolously, without any consideration for her own needs as well. Woman, don't hand over all your income to a husband who is not responsible for the family upkeep, children's school fees, household bills, etc. or who spends all the money on riotous living - drinking, womanizing, etc. Wisdom is profitable to direct (Eccl.10:10). Your attitude must, however, remain humble and nonconfrontational. Commitment on the woman's part also demands that she respects her husband. I am yet to find a man who hates to be respected! Lack of respect for the husband is what makes some men engage in physical combat with their wives (although this is not to justify such action). How some women address their husbands show they lack an understanding of family government as ordained by God. Woman, respect is reciprocal; it's give and take. If you give respect, you will earn respect. For instance, some wives are too "modern" to greet their husbands. He wakes up in the morning, and she's staring at him; no word of greetings. But she greets everyone else outside, with a smile for that matter. First get committed to the success of your marriage, and then you will get God committed.

Dedicated to Three Realms

Man is a spirit with a soul who inhabits a body. Man is tripartite, to put it another way. If it is accurate, which it is, it indicates that God anticipates marriage commitment to have an impact on the three spheres of spirit, soul, and body. Any union must comprehend this for it to be successful. Be devoted to your family's spiritual needs spiritually. Husbands, you are the family's high priest and prophet. You are to assume responsibility for the family's spiritual health. Spend some time in prayer for your family, and if necessary, consider fasting. Set a good example for your family by being devoted to God and the work of the kingdom. Spend time praying and studying God's Word with your family. Wives, you hold the family together spiritually. Since you were designed to have keen perception, you can pick up on things that others cannot. Be committed to bringing such matters before God in prayer during those times. It is impossible to overstate the importance of the Wesleys' mother's tale. It is known that she engaged every youngster in daily prayer, conversation, and good relationships. Therefore, her children could not fail to fulfill their roles in destiny. For future generations, her dedication to her family has paid off. A husband and wife should be dedicated to the mental growth of their family on both a mental and emotional level. Teach the kids the proper path to mental brilliance. Buy them books and other educational resources that will advance their mental dignity as an investment in their mental growth. Please refrain from purchasing items that will poison their minds in an effort to keep up with the latest fashion. If family success is to be achieved, the wellness of the family must physically receive the highest attention that it requires. If you deny your family the necessities of life, you cannot expect them to succeed. Do your best to guarantee that your family receives the best care possible. In the name of Jesus, you will succeed!

CHAPTER 7

CAN I TRUST YOU?

Trust is a crucial component of our family's everyday path. Without it, no family can achieve true success. Someone once stated that trust is defined as communication plus commitment plus time. A culture of efficient communication and dedication fosters trust. In a family where communication and devotion have stood the test of time, there is trust. Trust requires work and time. It is easily broken and difficult to fix, but if you are prepared to put in the effort necessary to make it work, the payoff is the prosperous family of your dreams.

What is faith?

Trust is a strong belief in someone's dependability, truth, or strength; a self-assured expectation, obligation, or responsibility; or the quality of being able to rely on someone.

Because of this, the psalmist referred to the Lord as "my rock, my fortress, and my deliverer" in Psalms 18:2. He also described him as "my God, my strength, in whom I will trust," "my buckler, and the horn of my salvation, and my high tower."

Trust, in a practical sense, is having faith that someone will treat you fairly, be loyal to you, and not desert you. Trust is something you cannot touch, taste, see, smell, or hear, but it has a profound impact on every successful family and every person who aspires to one. Trust is a component of every day existence. We put our trust in the fact that what we anticipate will happen every time we turn a switch, sit in a chair, or turn a doorknob. Many times, we don't even need to fast or pray before we accomplish these things. Why? Over time, we've realized that these items react to human touch in a natural way. No one can give you trust. It is a quality acquired over time and with experience. Trust is a two-way street. Members of your household will respond to you with trust more and more as you express it to them. When you decide to do so with God's miraculous assistance, you can also restore trust in strained relationships. Trust develops gradually. It takes time to establish trust, therefore you must demonstrate to your spouse both your own reliability and your own faith in them.

"God is a buckler to all who trust in him," it is said. "His path is faultless; the word of the LORD is proved." 18:30 in Psalms

Even God's Word must first be tested before faith can be established in it, and this process takes time. The same holds true for creating a happy family. Every member of your family must be able to respond to one another honestly at some time in your family relationship. If you constantly question the true intentions of other family members and rephrase their remarks and/or acts to suit your own agenda, you cannot have a successful family.

Why Believe?

Trust is essential to life itself. You trust that you will wake up the next morning, so you go to bed at night with a perfect plan for the following day. You eat food with the assurance that it will be digested by your body. You go to work each day with the conviction that the position you closed yesterday is still there and ready for you. You exhale freely without thinking to double-check the air's oxygen content or quality. Because of trust, all of these actions are carried out without hesitation. No successful family relationship can endure in a setting where there is no mutual trust. A married couple needs to develop trust. You must be able to trust your spouse with your past, present, and future if you want your marriage to last. Marriage depends on having the assurance that your partner loves and accepts you for who you are. You can unwind and let down your guard when you are aware that you are loved exactly as you are. It encourages openness without worrying about being rejected, and that is satisfying.

Proverbs 31:11's appropriate description of one of the attributes of the upright lady is this: "The heart of her husband doth safely trust in her, so that he shall need no spoil."

He is sure that his wife can be relied upon to handle specific family-related concerns. Due to this, my husband once came to my workplace and gave me a book of blank checks that were all signed. He could trust me to handle the money in that account because he had found me to be reliable when it came to handling money and didn't have to worry about his decision. Children who are born into homes where trust is openly demonstrated mature emotionally more steadily than those who are born into a dishonest environment. They tackle problems with sound judgment and have greater life confidence. Today, we have a lot of kids involved in all kinds of vices because we lack the crucial element of trust. Since they do not experience their parents' trust, they could care less if anyone else does. When there is no need for it, they become exceedingly self-defensive and defiant.

How To Build Trust

If trust is this important, then how do you build it? Trust does not naturally happen between two people or members of a family, even though they love each other. It takes work and a commitment to build. Your past experiences sometimes may affect your ability to trust. If you had been hurt in the past, it can be especially difficult. The good news, however, is that in Christ there is hope, for:

"...All things are by the law purged with blood ..." -Hebrews 9:22

The blood of Jesus was shed to cleanse us of all forms of unrighteousness, which includes all our past hurts and disappointments. If we will let God, He will eliminate all our past and give us the grace, strength and courage to build trust once again. Remember, we are all growing into perfection. So be quick to forgive your spouse or other members of your household when there has been a disappointment of expectations. In building trust, you need to be truthful. Be truthful to your spouse and family members. Don't be found to say one thing today and another tomorrow on the same issue. There is no substitute for truth! Your yea must be found to be yea, and your nay found to be nay. If you are a person with double standards, it becomes difficult to trust you. Even with your children, always say what you mean. The home becomes an untrustworthy environment when people make threats or say things they don't mean. They become empty words. So all the, "I will beat you" threats you issue to your children that have become a play sentence will only destroy their level of trust in your words and person. It is very important that members of your household can trust what you say. It is only men of truth that are considered for positions of responsibility.

"Moreover thou shalt provide out of all the people able men, such as fear God, men of truth, hating covetousness; and place such over them, to be rulers of thousands, and rulers of hundreds, rulers of fifties, and rulers of tens." -Exodus 18:21

Effective rulership of your family can only be established when members of the household know your commitment to truth. Truth commands and compels respect. Truth is a defense. Your integrity will speak for you in the day of adversity. It was what happened with Hezekiah when he was to die before he fulfilled the number of his days. He cried to God thus:

"... O LORD, remember now how I have walked before thee in truth and with a perfect heart, and have done that which is good in thy sight..." -2 Kings 20:3

God had to send Isaiah back to him, to inform him of the extension of his life by another fifteen years. The level of your boldness with your children will be greatly enhanced when they can trust you with the truth at all times. Another way to build trust is by keeping your promises to your family members. Promises have a way of creating excitement. It brings anticipation and hope, and if not kept, destroys trust. If for any reason you are not able to keep one, ensure that a thorough and honest explanation is given for it. Particularly in child raising, hope and trust in God and the society can be built or destroyed by our level of commitment to the fulfillment of our promises to our children. Don't make promises you know you will not fulfill, just to get your children off your back. Children find it very difficult to understand why a parent will promise to do something and fail to do so. Learn to follow the example that God has left for us.

"Blessed be the Lord, that hath given rest unto his people Israel, according to all that he promised: there hath not failed one word of all his good promise, which he promised by the hand of Moses his servant." -1 Kings 8:56

"They looked unto him, and were lightened: and their faces were not ashamed." Psalms 34:5

You will not know shame in your family, in Jesus' name! It is very important that spouses in a marriage respect, appreciate, and fulfill their marriage vows to each other. That is the only way to build trust. Remember that trust is built over a period of time. It is in the keeping of your vows to one another that trust is built. Trust cannot thrive in a home where there is no respect or regard for each other and the vows of marriage binding you to each other. When you deal treacherously with your spouse, even God is offended (Mal. 2:14).

Also, building trust demands that you be loyal to your spouse, especially in his/her absence. Loyalty breeds trustworthiness. The word loyal is defined by the American Heritage Dictionary to mean "steadfast in allegiance to one's home... faithful to a person, ideal, custom, cause, or duty." Loyalty means a feeling or attitude of devoted attachment and affection. It means faithfulness to a person or a cause." In other words, loyalty demands that your allegiance to your spouse and family must be in place, in order for you to build a successful family. Don't betray any of your family members. Betrayal destroys trust. For instance, as a mother, when your children trust you with some information, it is not for you to make it the subject of your dinner time conversation. A child in that situation will find it very difficult to entrust you with any other information he/she considers private and confidential.

True friendship is also negatively affected when there is a betrayal of trust. Believe in each other, and tell each other the truth at all times. In building a successful family, there must be confident expectations that weaknesses or confidences will not be betrayed.

The story of Isaac and Rebekah in Genesis 27 shows us clearly the harmful effect of the destruction of trust between couples. Rebekah engineered Jacob to deceive Isaac, using the weakness of his sight to obtain his father's blessings. It is interesting to note that that was the last effective contribution Rebekah ever made to life. That is a great lesson to learn. Your light will not be put out in obscurity!

Talking about the loyalty of Jesus, a writer said: "When we look at Jesus, we see that He did not live with a sense of open options. He was steadfast in His allegiance to the will of His father in heaven. He was faithful to His twelve disciples, bearing with them through thick and thin. Long after you and I would have given up on them, He was loyal to them." Loyalty demands that whatever you can't say in the presence of a family member, you should not be found saying it in his/ her absence. In the same vein, what you will be ashamed to be identified with, don't say either in his/ her presence or absence. Another very vital key needed for the building of trust in a family is forgiveness. Forgiveness in a marriage and among family members is not just an admonition, but a commandment. It is so vital that no marriage or family can survive its absence. As members of a family, you must learn the act of forgiving one another.

"Forgiveness is another way of admitting, 'I'm human, I make mistakes, I want to be granted that privilege, and so I grant you that privilege.' "

None of us is without sin. The Bible says in Romans 3:23-24: "For all have sinned and fall short of the glory of God; Being justified freely by his grace through the redemption that is in Christ Jesus." You are not always right yourself; you are only right in your own eyes. The Psalmist realising this, in Psalms 19:13 prayed earnestly to be delivered from presumptuous sins. You are only a product of grace. That is why the Bible says:

"Every way of a man is right in his own eyes: but the Lord pondereth the hearts." -Proverbs 21:2

"The way of a fool is right in his own eyes: but he that hearkeneth unto counsel is wise." -Proverbs 12:15

If God were to consider your own misdemeanors, where would you stand? "If thou, Lord, shouldest mark iniquities, O Lord, who shall stand? -Psalms 130:3

Since we are to be like Christ, then our forgiveness should be based on a new standard: one that grants forgiveness unconditionally, without the requirement of payment or the promise of change. Jesus, hanging from the cross in Luke 23:34, looked at the same people who had crucified Him and could still say: "Father, forgive them; for they know not what they do." And to the thief on the cross, who by simple expression of faith in Him in Luke 23:43,

He said: " ... Today you shalt be with me in paradise." That's unconditional forgiveness! There was no time for the thief to change first, before he could enjoy the forgiveness he needed to get into heaven. Jesus declared forgiveness and reconciliation without any conditions to be met. This is the right approach to forgiveness, in building trust in a marriage and among family members. It is the dimension of forgiveness my husband refers to humourously as "advance forgiveness". Seek to know and experience Christ's love and forgiveness in your own life, and that will make it easy for you to make a choice to forgive others. In building a successful family, all issues that have caused hurts, bitterness and resentments must be resolved daily before you go to bed, so you can rise up in the morning on a fresh note.

See what the Bible says: "Be ye angry, and sin not: let not the sun go down upon your wrath." -Ephesians 4:26

"Looking diligently lest any man fail of the grace of God; lest any root of bitterness springing up trouble you, and thereby many be defiled." -Hebrews 12:15

Bitterness embitters destiny, flee from it! Many people are well dressed, but rotten within, because of bitterness.

Unforgiveness is the root of bitterness, and it destroys. Forgiveness is its medicine! It is the wisdom of God.

Lastly in building trust, you must be accountable. Accountability is defined as "responsible: responsible to somebody else or to others, or responsible for something." Each member of the family must be conscious of the fact that they owe other members accountability in the handling of the affairs of the family, bearing in mind that even God will demand accountability from us.

"So then every one of us shall give account of himself to God." -Romans 14:12

Whatever your placement in the family, whether as father, mother or children, there are things for which God will hold you personally responsible. Like I said earlier in this book, there is a purpose for which God made you a member of that family. He expects you to fulfill that purpose, and will hold you accountable for the non-performance of that task. Accountability begins with the readiness to be held accountable for your actions. One major challenge of building a successful family is the vice of self-justification. No one wants to accept responsibility for anything that has gone wrong. There is always someone else to blame for our actions or inactions. The graphic picture painted in the Garden of Eden is very illustrative of this point: "And the LORD God called unto Adam, and said unto him, Where art thou? And he said, I heard thy voice in the garden, and I was afraid, because I was naked; and I hid myself. And he said, Who told thee that thou wast naked? Hast thou eaten of the tree, whereof I commanded thee that thou shouldest not eat? And the man said, The woman whom thou gavest to be with me, she gave me of the tree, and I did eat. And the LORD God said unto the woman, What is this that thou hast done? And the woman said, The serpent beguiled me, and I did eat." -Genesis 3:9-13

That is the nature of the fallen man. Perhaps the path to redemption would have taken a different cause had Adam simply accepted responsibility for his action and sought forgiveness. God is plenteous in mercy; just maybe Jesus would not have needed to pay the ultimate price of death to reconcile us back to God. Sometimes some families have had to go through hard times, and in some cases, suffer some irreparable losses, just because one of the members refused to accept responsibility.

Responsibility is a sign of maturity. Until you are matured enough to be accountable for rights and wrongs done, you cannot be said to be responsible enough to handle the affairs of life. Life itself is a product of personal responsibility. I am appalled when I find or counsel people who blame their kith and kin or the society or economy for their failures. Life will only answer to you when you are ready to accept responsibility for what it will take to make it work. The same is true of building a successful family. Trust in a family can only be built when each member, particularly the parents, are matured enough to take the lead in accepting responsibility for making the family a place of honour and dignity. Children who grow up in a home where the parents are ready to accept responsibility and where there is an open expression of apology for all irresponsible acts tend to also live responsible lives. In raising your children, one of the virtues they should find in you is accountability. The goal for accountability is for us to grow strong and take responsibility for our lives.

The focus must be growth, not just preservation. Accountability is always mutual. Parents must realise that they are accountable to their children too. When you give account to members of your family, they also feel compelled to be accountable. Trust, respect, honour, love and submission grow as we become more accountable.

The goals, objectives, strategies, and means for communicating accountability must be made clear for it to be effective. Every member of the family must understand the need to be accountable one to another. For instance, a man must realise that trust is built when he lets members of his family know his whereabouts at all times, even if it is around the neighbourhood. He should not just run into a friend on the way and decide to follow him home without first telling someone in his household his whereabouts. The same goes for every member of the household. All forms of suspicions are eliminated in a family setup this way. In this wild and evil world we live in today, accidents or losses can be avoided this way. Several people have lost their lives to such careless and unaccountable movements. Even their family members could not trace their corpses, because they had no idea where to look. Sometimes, people are not even sure whether the person is dead or still alive. Clear lines of accountability should be well defined to all members of the family. Every member of the family must also be made to realise the specific responsibilities for which they will be held accountable. For instance, it should be clearly understood by all that the father is the head of the family union. The mother is known to be the manager of the family affairs, and the children also have certain responsibilities to fulfill such as household chores, a commitment to school or work, whichever applies at their level, and so on. This type of clarity allows trust to be built and prevents self-justification. Sometimes, there is a breakdown of accountability when family members are assigned responsibilities and the needed authority to make it work is not provided. Every member of the family, particularly the parent in the home, must effectively stand in their positions of authority in the home government to ensure accountability. Time and avenues should also be provided for everyone to give an account of the responsibilities given to them per time. It is only human to take seriously a responsibility for which you know you will be checked. Not everyone is good at working without supervision. In building a successful family, therefore, the aim of accountability is to teach every member of the family to take personal responsibility for their actions and be conscious of the subsequent effect of these actions on the entire family.

Trust's Advantages

Because it fosters an atmosphere for intimacy to develop between family members, trust is essential to creating a successful family. Only with trust as its foundation can true and enduring intimacy be built. Intimacy takes time to develop; it is not something that happens naturally and cannot be forced. It is similar to how trust takes time to develop. Only in situations where everyone involved has a strong sense of security and confidence in the other people's moral character will intimacy flourish.

The definition of intimacy is "a sense of intimacy and belonging; closeness in friendship or acquaintance." What trust does for a family is bring everyone closer together, giving them a genuine sense of belonging in a setting of true friendship.

The Lord's blessings are unavoidably required for an intimate family. Because: "Look, what a pleasant and good thing it is for brothers to dwell together in unity... for there the LORD commanded the blessing, even life for evermore." - Psalms 133: 1, 3

Truly intimate environments tend to produce very emotionally balanced children. Due to the overwhelming love and affection they receive from their family members, they find it easier to resist and withstand peer pressure because there is no unfulfilled void in their lives. Physical and emotional contact are necessary for intimacy. Emotional closeness among family members fosters an honest and open exchange of feelings, experiences, and thoughts.

Second, trust drives out fear.

The LORD is my strength and my song; he has also become my salvation. "Behold, God is my salvation; I will trust, and I will not be afraid." (Isaiah 12:2)

Eliminating fear is arguably one of the biggest advantages of trust in creating a successful family. In a family setting, fear is a spirit that gives birth to jealousy and insecurity. The peace in the family is destroyed by these. A feeling of agitation and anxiety brought on by the existence or imminence of danger is referred to as fear. Sometimes a sense of insecurity among family members causes an unjustified suspicion of marital infidelity. This can be gotten rid of with trust.

In addition, "firm reliance on the integrity, ability, or character of a person or thing" is another definition of trust. The spirit of fear is completely eradicated from the family structure when the honesty of family members can be confirmed. In any family, strength comes with the absence of fear. A family's ability to cooperate to solve problems is strengthened by members' confidence in their morality and character. Their Christian testimony's secret lies in the power of family unity.

The LORD is my rock, my fortress, and my deliverer. He is my God, my strength, and the one I will put my trust in. He is also my buckler, the horn of my salvation, and my high tower. -Psalm 18:2

Please take note that it takes time and patience to establish trust. It is a virtue that must be actively developed; it is not a gift. It all starts with you.

CHAPTER 8

DWELL IN CONFORMITY WITH KNOWLEDGE

Family members' incomplete understanding of their God-given roles within the family structure is the primary source of today's family difficulties. One cannot do something they do not understand. A person cannot carry out his responsibilities in the context of the family if he is unaware of them. I'll be looking at one of the crucial tasks needed to succeed as a family in this chapter.

The Bible says in 1 Peter 3:7 that husbands should live with their wives "according to knowledge, paying honor to the wife, as unto the weaker vessel, and as being heirs together of the grace of life," so that their prayers won't be impeded.

The words "Dwell with them according to knowledge" are highlighted in this passage. The Greek word "sunoikeo," which is used to refer to domestic association, is translated as "dwell"; nonetheless, this association must be made sensibly. Understanding the characteristics and responsibilities of each family member is necessary for any family to be successful in any way. So what exactly is knowledge? "the state or fact of knowing; familiarity, awareness, or understanding gained by experience or study; precise information about something" is the definition of knowledge. Therefore, when the Bible commands us to "dwell by knowledge," it means that there are specific facts that one must grasp in order to enjoy success in one's family. When we are unaware of our responsibilities in achieving God's ultimate goal for the family, there are many family problems that arise.

Hosea 4:6 in the Bible states, "My people are destroyed through lack of knowledge."

For success to abound in the family, each family member must carry out a specific duty given to them by God. One of our family's success factors, knowledge acquisition, is something my husband and I frequently discuss. He started asking God what His true intent was for the institution of marriage as a result of what he seen with regard to it during his formative years. God revealed to him the seven principles of marriage during this time, and our family has successfully implemented these principles by doing so. It took knowledge for us to understand where we each fit within the family network, and that understanding has freed us from all family crises.

In order to achieve family success, the importance of information cannot be overstated.

A house is built by wisdom, and through understanding, it is established; with knowledge, its chambers are filled with priceless treasures, according to Proverbs 24:3–4, which lists the advantages of knowledge.

Knowledge is the key if you want to identify homes (families) that are brimming with precious and lovely treasures of joy, happiness, satisfaction, sunshine, fulfillment, etc. To live successful family life, one needs knowledge. God is the origin of the advice to live in the family network in accordance with knowledge.

In light of the fact that the Bible states in Proverbs 2:6 that "the LORD gives wisdom," knowledge and understanding "come from his mouth," I will be examining His instruction on the matter.

In the Bible, the terms wisdom, knowledge, and understanding are frequently used interchangeably. However, they are occasionally described as being different and separate. Knowing what to do next is wisdom; knowledge is having the facts; understanding is being able to extract meaning from the facts. The capacity for information gathering and access is known as knowledge. Unless the data gathered is understood, which directs you to the next course of action, this alone might not be helpful. Wisdom is the capacity to determine which principles to apply in this moment. Understanding, on the other hand, is the capacity to extract meaning from information, which produces principles. Without an awareness of one's obligations and a commitment to fulfilling them, the command to dwell according to knowledge will not be fruitful. Therefore, this chapter is devoted to the biblical guidance given to husbands, wives, and children regarding their covenant obligations, blessings, and privileges.

the men's obligations

"Men, love your wives, and be not bitter against them," the Bible commands husbands. – Colossians 3:19

For the same reason, "you husbands, dwell with them according to understanding, paying honor to the wife, as unto the weaker vessel, and as being heirs jointly of the grace of life; that your prayers be not hindered." -1 Peter 3:7

"Husbands, treat your wives with respect and affection, just as Christ did for the church, for whom he gave his life. Men should therefore respect their spouses' bodies just as much as their own. Whoever loves his wife, loves himself. Because nobody has ever hated their own flesh; instead, they nourish and cherish it, just like the Lord the church." Ephesians 5:25–29

To provide for and generally monitor the wellbeing of his family is a man's principal duty in the family. The man has a heavy burden to love his wife as Christ loves the Church, and he is not excused from this duty even if his wife is unrepentant or unbelieving. Only through making sacrifices, setting a godly example, and having an unwavering devotion to his family can he fulfill this role. Second only to God, your wife is your first focus.

This kind of love is nicely described in Matthew 5:43–48. In that passage, Jesus commanded us to model human love after the way God loves. Both the just and the unjust receive God's rain, and both the good and the evil receive God's sun. This kind of love is gentle and unwaveringly compassionate. It will never look out for anything but the best interests of the family. In the same way, regardless of how other family members act, the guy must always look out for their best interests. The guy is the head of the home and is in charge of the entire family. He has a big obligation as the union's leader to safeguard, look out for, and work for his family's whole well-being—spiritually, physically, and emotionally. Love of this nature must be demonstrated in deeds, not just in words. A man can tell his family members that he loves them all day long, but until he acts on that love, his words won't accomplish much to improve the bond between them. This aspect of love also requires that, regardless of how people treat him, he always treat them right. The spouse should support the spiritual growth of his family in the same way that Christ supported the spiritual growth of His disciples. He must be willing to do anything, including risking his life, to protect them. This involves giving up selfish interests and pastimes that keep him from the family or use up valuable funds from the family budget. The spouse must also lead his family in Bible study and frequent family devotions if he wants to see their family's spiritual growth. In particular, he is to lead by example in the worship of God. In addition, a man cannot manage his family's affairs before engaging in daily Bible study and prayerful fellowship with the Lord. The personal knowledge of your wife and family members is also a part of what it is to "live with them according to knowledge." Intimacy grows from familiarity.

The husband must invest the time and effort to learn what his wife and family members enjoy and detest, what brings them joy and sorrow, and what gives them security and insecurity. He must then work to satisfy or appease them. A man should have compassion for his family's needs and emotions. Their mental and physical needs must always be taken into account. I concur with a wise man when he said that the more we know about God, the more we will love Him and be more loyal to and obedient to Him. The family is similar in this regard. A man will love his family more and want to help and care for them if he has a better understanding of their needs. Studying God's Word diligently is the only way to gain the necessary knowledge in each of these fields (2 Tim.2:15).

The respect a man must have for his wife and other family members is another important obligation. Perhaps even more responsibility is involved here than merely meeting their physical needs. It is said that respect is mutual. A guy must be willing to put some effort into earning the respect of his family if he wants to enjoy it. His family must be revered, admired, valued, praised, and exalted. These he accomplishes through his chaste behavior, words, and conduct. A man will undoubtedly benefit from his family's chaste speech if he is soft spoken with them. A man with a stern disposition will undoubtedly create a family that is stern and nagging.

An ideal man should not be a despot. Even though they perform different roles, a man and his wife are equal before God. Wives and husbands are to submit to one another (Col. 3:18, 1Pet. 3:1-7). It should be highlighted that women are neither less valuable or less important than men. Although a woman is equal to her husband, the marriage vow requires her to submit to him even though she is of equal rank to other males (Gen. 24:8, 58). So it becomes simple for a guy to honor his wife if he acknowledges this crucial fact.

the women's obligations

The wives are instructed to submit to their own husbands as the Lord would have them do. – Colossians 3:18

They do this in order to "teach the young women to be sober, to love their husbands, to love their children, to be discreet, chaste, keepers at home, good, obedient to their own husbands, that the word of God be not blasphemed." -Titus 2:4-5 "Wives, submit to your husbands as you would the Lord. Because Christ is the head of the church and the savior of the body, the husband is the wife's primary caregiver. So let the ladies submit to their own husbands in every way, just as the church is subject to Christ." – Ephesians 5:22–24

After the Lord, the woman's spouse and children are her major sources of obligation. In Genesis 2, the woman was given the title "help meet," which made it obvious that she should support her husband as the head of the household.

According to the Bible, women must submit to men in all matters. A wise man named David Lipscomb wrote, "The wife submits to her husband with love, respect, and reverence, which is appropriate given the relationship they share. While he is the husband, he is the obvious, scripturally established head of the family and is on an equal spiritual footing with her in that regard. Nothing is expected of her that is contrary to her Christian character; rather, her submission must be in accordance with the standards of righteousness." In order to live according to knowledge and have a successful family, a woman must recognize and use her understanding of her place in the family.

Because they associate submission with inferiority, many women have trouble understanding the concept of submission. God created both men and women equally, but for the purposes of His plan of salvation, He gave each of them certain duties to fulfill. God has expressly commanded the lady to obey her own husband. That is the plan that God envisioned for her blessings. In the lines mentioned above, the subject of surrender is very clearly expressed. The wife must obey her husband. The husband should be the wife's primary provider, and submission should be made in a way that pleases the Lord. The Church's submission to Christ serves as an example for how everything else should be done. God created women to play that role in the family structure. When goal is unknown, abuse is inevitable, according to a wise man's saying. Women struggle to submit because they are unsure of why it is necessary or how to accomplish it.

Because "the husband is the head of the wife," Ephesians 5:23 makes clear why submission is necessary.

That is the divine design and purpose. The wife should submit to her husband, who is the head, in the same way that a body submits to the brain in the head, which is where it is supposed to be. A deformity or something out of the ordinary is visible when you observe a body that is not responsive to the head. You notice a dysfunctional individual. In a marriage, the same holds true. Distortion, deformity, and malfunction result when a wife refuses to submit to her husband. God created the body to respond to the head, and the husband is the wife's head. As Christ is the head of the church, verse 23 provides the example of submission: In other words, a wife must submit to her husband in the same way that the Church does to Christ. In order for the wife to succeed in her family, she must submit to her husband with the same wholehearted, unreserved, joyful, and willing heart that the Church has in obeying Christ. Women should carefully seek the Lord and make an effort to act, behave, and dress in a chaste manner. The woman has a responsibility to look for volunteer opportunities in appropriate capacities and to develop the skills required for caring for her home. Because Sarah submitted to Abraham, the Lord found her to be pleasing, and as a result, Sarah gave birth to numerous nations.

The purpose of the woman was to aid man in his endeavors and produce offspring to populate the earth. According to the book of Titus, the woman also has a duty to love her husband and her children, to be sensible and morally upright, and to be morally and sexually faithful to her husband in every way. The woman should also be more focused on who she is than how she looks. According to First Timothy 2:9–10, a woman should be modest and discreet in her appearance, exhibiting godly fear while remaining sober and modest. Being a worker at home is one of the woman's additional responsibilities in her household. She is a "keeper at home," according to Titus 2:5. This isn't just a reference to the fact that she cleans the bathrooms, sweeps the floors, and so forth. It simply implies that her work, in whatever capacity, takes place at home. It's not that a woman must always be busy at home or that she isn't allowed to leave the house to work or engage in other activities. Not that she has to do household chores and menial tasks all the time. It simply means that her divine mission is to fulfill it in the home. The woman has been given by God the responsibility of maintaining the home. God won't accomplish for you what you were created to do. The woman is expected to maintain the home, care for her husband, and make sure that their children and husband have everything they need to live comfortably.

She is expected to provide her family with a comfortable and happy life using the resources her husband brings home. She must impart to her children the spiritual knowledge and lessons she acquires. She maintains order at home. She must acknowledge that she has a duty to pray for the family. None of the others will if she doesn't. You are the only person who can pray for your family with the same fervor. You are in the best position to know what to do to keep your home free from all kinds of evil because only you truly understand its true condition. My husband frequently attests that he hasn't given our home his undivided attention because I've always taken my responsibility as the housekeeper seriously. I've always taken what my husband offers, such as the mission of the ministry God has entrusted to him, and given it to the kids and to every other member of our family. No issue has ever arisen because everyone always knows where to fit in. In Jesus' name, that will also serve as your witness.

Children's Responsibilities

The guys were the ones who were particularly instructed to "live according to wisdom." However, for families to succeed, kids must also understand their obligations to their parents. According to Ephesians 6:1-3, "Obey your parents in the Lord, kids; that is the correct thing to do. The first commandment with a promise is to honor your parents so that everything will go well for you and you can live a long time on this planet." It is a commandment to honor your parents. According to this verse, it is actually the first commandment with a promise attached. Even though they work extremely hard, many people nowadays still struggle to succeed in life. This may be because they have disgraced their parents. God's command must be obeyed if you desire to experience good. A commandment that is inviolable is to honor and respect your parents. It doesn't have any predetermined conditions under which it can be disobeyed. So, regardless of your parents' state —good, awful, insensitive, unreasonable, born again, etc.—you must show them respect. According to the dictionary, honor is defined as "esteem owed or paid to merit; high regard; respect; attention; reverence; veneration; show of respect or reverence." This means that, in all situations, you should treat your parents with the respect and reverence they deserve and hold them in high regard. Reuben lost his prestigious position in destiny as a result of his refusal to honor his father.

Genesis 35:22 from the Bible reports: Reuben went to sleep with Bilhah, his father's concubine, and Israel found out about it when they were living there.

When Jacob blessed his sons in Genesis 49:3–4, Reuben received the following blessings: "Reuben, you are my firstborn, my strength and the source of my might, the height of honor and the pinnacle of authority: You won't succeed since you polluted your father's bed by climbing up to my couch after defiling his bed, making you as unstable as water." It is regrettable because Reuben exemplified dignity by fate. His destiny called for him to be a man of honor. However, he lost it due to a single act of dishonor and disrespect for his father.

In Matthew 19:16–19, Jesus clarified this issue further. "As I watched, someone approached him and asked, "Good Master, what good act shall I do so that I may have eternal life?" He then addressed him with the following statement: But if you want to live, follow God's instructions. Which? he asks the person. Honour your parents, Jesus commanded." Life on earth and eternity with God are both correlated with the respect that children show for their parents. Exodus 20:12 records Moses receiving this as one of the Ten Commandments. A triple chord is not easily broken, according to Ecclesiastes 4:12 of the Bible.

As a youngster in a family, respect for your parents is non-negotiable if you want to live a long and happy life. In Jesus' name, you will succeed!

CHAPTER 9

REPAIRING THE CRACKS

Lizards find it comfortable to hide in the cracks in a house's walls. The lizards of life can be compared to the devil and his minions, and marriage, as I have said throughout this book, is like a house. You're giving the devil free entry to your house if you allow even a small crack.

Nor do they allow the devil to enter. - Ephesians 4:27

The importance of commitment to a successful family life has already been established. Without commitment, trust cannot be built, and without trust, marriage problems can arise. Unfilled cracks develop into gullies, and gullies eventually transform into canyons due to erosion. In other words, any gap you ignore will enlarge over time until separation is unavoidable.

Keep an eye on the forgiving!

Today, one of the biggest gaps in many families' walls is unforgiveness. Couples who experience this tend to cling to old grudges and hurts, and eventually a rift that is so wide that it splits the family develops. I compare family dysfunction and unforgiveness to cancer. I refer to it as "family cancer." In the same way that cancer devours the body, unforgiveness has devoured and torn apart many families.

"Looking carefully lest any man fall from the grace of God; lest any root of bitterness springing up trouble you, lest many be polluted by it." (Hebrews 12:15)

Bitterness and unforgiveness have no place in your life. Learn to pardon each other without delay. Even before offenses are committed, you can take it a step further by learning to forgive.

One intriguing aspect of anger and bitterness is that, unlike the person you are angry with, you are the one who ends up paying the price.

In fact, it is a proven medical fact that when you are angry, bitter, or live in unforgiveness, your body system is set at an imbalance that eventually leads to the demise of your health. One minute of sadness reduces immunity by six hours, while one minute of laughter increases immunity by twenty-four hours, according to a researcher. So pay attention to what God says and develop the ability to pull every root of resentment and offense out of your life before it has a chance to destroy you.

Going too far in forgiving

Allow me to say that wisdom demands that you not put your life in danger in the name of forgiveness when we are talking about it. She needs to use caution in this situation if the man has been abusive, has threatened to kill her, or has actually made attempts to do so. Get out of there quickly if you find yourself in that situation! However, if you are in an abusive relationship even though your life is not in danger, seek advice from Spirit-filled, born-again marriage counselors. In Jesus' name, you will be protected.

Put Your Relationship in Writing

An unauthorized union is another gap that might harm your family's prosperity. Without a legal marriage—that is, without dowries or other forms of formal engagement—some couples have been cohabitating for years and have even had children together. A formal wedding was conducted in the Garden of Eden, as is abundantly clear from the account of the first marriage in Genesis 2. When Eve was wandering around in another area of the garden, Adam did not just pick her up, bring her home, and they immediately began living together. The Bible says that God "... brought her unto the man" in verse 22. To give her to Adam, God had to intervene physically.

The family is built upon marriage. You need to be married before you can enjoy a prosperous family. If you haven't already, pay the dowry. According to the Bible, dowries must be paid in some way. The fact that you practice Christianity does not excuse you from paying the parents' debt.

Render to Caesar what is Caesar's, and to God what is God's, the Bible says in Mark 12:17 in response to their question.

Assume that the bride's family is entitled to the dowry payment, and make sure to honor that request. A very graphic description of an average wedding and everything that must be done is found in the book of Genesis. To find Isaac a wife from among his brothers, Abraham sent his servant. The servant found Rebekah because God made his travels successful.

In Genesis 24:51–53 of the Bible, the following is mentioned: "Rebekah is here; take her and go; make her the wife of the son of your master, as the LORD has commanded. And so it happened that after hearing what they had to say, Abraham's servant bowed down to the ground in worship of the LORD. The servant then brought out precious items for Rebekah, including clothing, silver and gold jewelry, and other gifts. He also gave Rebekah's mother and brother valuable items." Laban, who was now serving as the family's head, and Rebekah's mother were both given valuable items, as you can see. You should be careful about the items you present as dowry when paying the dowry, I must emphasize. It is never advisable to say anything that could compromise your Christian testimony. I can still clearly recall what transpired before my marriage to my husband. The list of items my parents gave my husband to bring as dowry included some things that would have an impact on our Christian testimony. The items on the list were simply removed after my husband spoke with them about how such an action might affect us in the future in light of the Bible. The future of a daughter is something that no parent wants to risk. A proper word spoken in due season is all that is necessary. How powerful are right words? the Bible exclaims. (Job

6:25).

Your parents will listen to you if you speak to them in the right way, I'm sure of it. You only need to ask the Holy Spirit for assistance if you want to speak correctly and be aware of appropriate cues. You can convince them to support you if you do it that way.

You must make sure you have parental approval after you have completed all the necessary steps. When your parents bestow blessings on you, for some reason, those blessings stick with you until all of their good intentions are realized in your life. Rebekah wasn't simply taken away by Abraham's servant.

In Genesis 24:58–60, the Bible reports: "When Rebekah was called, they asked if she would accompany the man. I'm going, she continued. Rebekah, their sister, along with her nurse, Abraham's servant, and his men, were dispatched. They praised Rebekah and told her, "You are our sister; be the mother of thousands of millions; and let thy seed possess the gate of those who hate you."" In fact, we are all a part of the thousands of millions of blessings that were predicted for Rebekah, and they all materialized in her life (Gal. 4:28). In the name of Jesus, you will additionally encounter this level of blessings.

Acknowledging the location of a holy Christian wedding is a crucial component of formalizing your marriage. God's actual participation in the institution of marriage is seen in Genesis 2:22. Adam received Eve from him. And the rib that the LORD God had removed from the man, he made into a woman and brought her to the man, according to the Bible.

Therefore, it will be dangerous to think that you can defeat the devil's attacks and wickedness on the institution of marriage without Him. According to Scripture (Rev. 12:12; 2 Timothy 3:1), the devil will act more wickedly in the last days. Because he understands that the family is essential to maintaining world peace, he is waging a fierce war against it. Due to this, families are dissolving at an alarming rate today.

Only a bastard would want to get married away from his father's home because God is your Father. Everything in life is different when God is present. Christian marriages take place with God being invited to participate and taking the center stage. It is impossible to ignore that. So make sure to have a traditional Christian wedding to formalize your union. It is crucial that you ask your pastor to bless your union if you are already cohabitating or were never wed in church. This is true even if you are unable to have an open church wedding like newlyweds can.

A proper legal record of your union must be kept on file, which is also crucial. God always makes sure that there is a token in His interactions with people so that the covenant's terms are constantly brought to mind. Genesis 8:20–22 and 9:14–17 mention the rainbow in relation to Noah. Genesis 17:9–11 describes Abraham's sacrificial experience. Even Jesus had the blood-sealed covenant of our salvation as evidence (Heb. 8:6).

Your legal spouse is not a safety device as the world would define one. It is merely a point of contact to remind God that you have completed all of the requirements for your marriage, so the enemy cannot enter your family. Formalizing your marriage with your spouse will assist cut down on various entry points that the devil might have used to infiltrate your household. Because of a leak in their home, many people work really hard yet end up with very little or nothing to show for it. Some even experience severe health issues as a result of the devil finding a reason to be against them.

According to the Bible, "Whoever makes a pit shall fall into it; and whoever makes a hedge, a serpent shall bite him" (Eccl. 10:8).

the instance of Job Only by letting some of his anxiety out could he let the devil in. He continued making sacrifices to appease God in order to avoid the curse since he was so continually terrified of the potential repercussions of his children's misdeeds (Job 1:5). He therefore uttered these words when tragedy struck: "For the thing which I greatly feared is come upon me, and that which I was scared of is come unto me" (Job 3:25). I once mentioned this truth at a gathering for women. Due of the lady's parents' opposition to their marriage, a couple who had been living together for almost ten years without being married and had three children decided to reconcile and act morally. They have seen significant financial ups and downs throughout the years. They make substantial investments yet receive little in return. They were covenant adherents who had a strong zeal for God's goods, yet they also fell into hell. After seeing the lady's family and paying the dowry, they headed to church where one of the pastors sanctified their union. Great commercial opportunities for them soon followed. Their way of living changed. Through the straightforward process of formalizing their union, they started to receive all kinds of favors, including the ability to build their own home and even purchase a Mercedes Benz vehicle! The following will be your personal testimonial! The offspring of such an unholy coupling likewise suffer the consequences of life. According to the Bible, parental sins continue to impact offspring up into the third and fourth generations (Deut. 5:9). Additionally, it is possible that children reared in these relationships will also end up in similar unions. Your children's contempt and disrespect for the institution of marriage will cause you enormous grief if you don't respect and value it. But just like that couple, take action right now to mend this covenant gap in your relationship.

CHAPTER 10

GET GOING

Success in your family is not only possible for you, it is a reality! Your relationship may have reached a stage where you feel like there is no hope left. Though not at all! You can ask for a second chance from God because He is the God of second chances.

It is possible to conclude from the Bible that families have no chance of surviving, particularly if you take Adam and Eve's story into account. However, the New Testament makes it clear that God still values the family. I think that's why the first miracle Jesus worked during His time on earth—the one that removed disgrace and brought about family restoration—was not one that opened closed eyes or healed the sick (Jn. 2:1-11).

Jesus showed His desire in turning tasteless marriages or families into sweet ones, common houses into miraculous ones, and colorless families into colorful ones by turning water into wine. But you have to make the first move. You must do as that bridegroom did and ask Jesus to be a part of your union. Make Him in charge of the celebration! In Nigeria, most homes used to have a popular plaque that said, "Christ is the Head of this family; the silent Listener to every discourse; the unseen Guest at every meal." These words highlight the reason why so many families fail. Christ continued to be the unseen Guest and silent Hearer. He is never allowed a voice in the matters of their houses, and neither is He ever given respect. No one loves to hang out in a place where they are not welcomed, and he is treated as an unwelcome guest. God never forces Himself upon anyone.

He said: "Look, I'm standing at the door and knocking. If any man hears my voice and opens the door, I'll go in to him and we'll eat together, and he with me" (Rev. 3:20).

At the door, he is waiting. Even though he knows that "with God, nothing is impossible," he refuses to enter (Lk.1:37).

He consistently awaits an invitation. Jesus must be welcomed into your home in order for your family to succeed. You must request His presence in your family in order to benefit from it, as only those who request are eligible to receive (Matthew 7:7). I implore you to make Jesus the Lord of your house so that He might display His glory there.

This invitation begins with a brief prayer that is spoken with heartfelt faith. Please say this prayer aloud if you would want to do that:

"I therefore declare You to be my Lord and Savior, O Lord Jesus Christ. Let Your blood cleanse me of my sins. I believe You died for me and rose from the dead on the third day so that I might be justified. As of right now, I consider myself to be a child of God, rescued, justified, forgiven, and justified. I'm grateful that You, Lord, saved me. Amen!"

Congratulations! With all the associated blessings the Bible mentions, you have now been born again and adopted as a child of God. You are invited to welcome Him to become the Lord of your home as you read this testimony and then join me in praying the next prayer.

"Dear Lord Jesus Christ, I now ask You to rule over my family because I have declared You to be my Lord and my Savior. I commend You for Your ongoing presence in this home and encourage You to assume complete control over the activities of this family. Amen. "Thank You, Lord " In Jesus' name, I foresee miracles happening in your home starting right now! Right today, every destroyed hedge has been rebuilt.

Your share is family success! I see God turning your grieving into dancing once more in whichever area you have cried and grieved with your family. God is intervening and will release you from captivity no matter what your family is going through right now.

Obedience to all of the instructions you have learned throughout the course of reading this book is another thing you should start with. Information is just that until it is put into practice. Scripture knowledge is merely information; it is only through practice that you can reap its rewards. Understanding and action should be sparked by knowledge.

According to James 1:22–25 in the Bible: "But avoid simply hearing the word and fooling yourself; rather, practice what you preach. Because if someone only hears the message without acting on it, he or she is like a person who sees a reflection of their natural face and immediately forgets what kind of person they were. But the person who continues to look at the perfect law of liberty and is not merely a hearer who forgets but a doer of the job will be blessed in his deed."

Until you act in accordance with God's word, you are merely fooling yourself. Only practitioners of The Word are effective. Your obedience must be eager and willing in order to yield results. God has imposed the need of willingness for anything to create results. Isaiah 1:19 in the Bible states, "If you are willing and obedient, you shall eat the good of the land."

Your marriage has some excellent aspects, but you'll need to eat them willingly. You will always receive a reward for any action you conduct in accordance with God's word.

In spite of all difficulties, God will always defend you if you choose to obey him and walk out in faith. So don't be frightened to act on everything you have learned from this book. God is committed to support you and provide you with a positive testimony. Your family's success can start today.

www.ingramcontent.com/pod-product-compliance
Lightning Source LLC
LaVergne TN
LVHW050601160826
845677LV00011B/2406

9798367226843